Live
Like
Louis!

Inspiring Stories
From the Life
Of Louis Armstrong
To Help You Lead
A More *Wonderful* Life

Phil Lynch

16th Street Press

16th Street Press
322 S. 16th Street, Escanaba, MI 49829

www.livelikelouis.com

Cover photo: Philippe Halsman, 1966
© Philippe Halsman/Magnum Photos

Back cover: William P. Gottlieb, 1946, public domain

In memory of my mother

Mary Anne Lynch

who surrendered her bankbook
to borrow money for her son's trombone

Bach said everything is in its place;
Armstrong said the sun comes shining through.

- Richard Brookhiser

Program

Live
Like
Louis!

Intro

*in which you and I become acquainted
and begin at the end of Louis's life*

I invite you to close your eyes and think of Louis
Armstrong. What comes to mind? If you picture
something, I'll bet it's Satchmo's huge smile. He
was indeed a happy man who enjoyed life with a
very positive outlook. When you think of Louis, do
you hear anything? Maybe you can hear his bois-
terous laugh or that warm, gravelly voice singing
"What a Wonderful World," the song that has become his anthem of sorts. It's an appropriate one for
him, since it pretty much summarizes his actual
outlook on life. As a musician, when I call him to
mind, I hear his lively early jazz playing that established him as a great soloist and the founding father
of "swing."

There are many facets to Louis Armstrong: jazz
icon, innovative singer, "pop" crossover artist, radio and movie star, globetrotting jazz ambassador,
and non-stop professional musician who toured
almost to his dying day. And of course there's Louis
Armstrong, the man. Whenever I would tell some-

one I was writing about Louis, literally each person would smile and say something positive about Louis or one of his songs. Even my high school students, even *they* feel positively about him, and they're "cool" teenagers! Years ago I was in the church business and someone advised me that you can talk about religion or your beliefs and really turn some people off. But talk about Jesus and pretty much everybody still likes *him*. I've found the same thing true with Louis: seriously, who dislikes Louis Armstrong? Moreover, a number of events and individuals in his fascinating life can serve to inspire us to be better people ourselves.

If you're not really into jazz or music history, you can rest easy: this isn't a book about music. It's a book about living. Someone once asked Louis if jazz was folk music. He replied, "All music is folk music. I ain't never heard no horse sing a song." I intend this book not for jazz fans or music buffs, but for folks, for anyone who can use a little inspiration to be a better person. If that's you (and I hope it is), I invite you to come along as we explore stories and people from the life of Louis Armstrong. I'll be careful not to give advice; I won't say, "Just do thus and such." I think it works better to offer reminders and examples of how we *can* be. So at the end of each chapter, you'll find personal growth practices to try if you wish. There are also suggested songs to listen to, with links available on the companion website, www.livelikelouis.com.

One of leadership expert Stephen Covey's famous seven habits of effective people is to begin with the end in mind. So, before we begin in chapter one to contemplate the difficult early surroundings Louis overcame, it's important we share an understanding of what he did with his life.

Accomplishments

I thought I knew "Pops" (the name his friends called him) pretty well. But while researching his life, I was really impressed by how "far out" Louis Armstrong really was. Or is. You see, he's still far out today, literally out of this world: one of his early recordings is on the Voyager spacecraft now leaving our solar system! I can think of no better representative of the human race. Some alien "cats" will be "diggin' ol' Satch" light years away some day.

But seriously, let's hear what experts have to say about Louis. *Time* named him one of its 100 most important people of the 20th century. That's people in general, not just entertainers. Filmmaker Ken Burns says, "Armstrong is to music what Einstein is to physics and the Wright Brothers are to travel." Gary Giddins, one of our best music critics, calls Armstrong "America's Bach." Duke Ellington, whom many would nominate as America's greatest composer, simply called Louis "Mister Jazz." Tony Bennett (himself a U.N. Citizen of the World) says, "The bottom line of any country in the world is 'What did we contribute to the world?' We contributed Louis Armstrong."

Halls of fame really like Louis. He's in at least eight including the Rock and Roll Hall of Fame (for his influence on the blues). That same hall includes his "West End Blues" as one of its 500 most influential recordings. Eleven of his records are in the Grammy Hall of Fame, and he won the Grammy Lifetime Achievement Award posthumously. Naturally, Louis has a star on that famous sidewalk in Hollywood.

Let's move back in time a bit. At Louis's passing in 1971, both the president and State Department issued public statements of condolence. Louis's honorary pallbearers included the governor of New York, the mayor of New York City, the aforementioned Duke of Ellington, plus Bing Crosby, Frank Sinatra, and Johnny Carson. At the time of his passing, Louis had played hundreds of dates a year for almost thirty years, including one in Ghana attended by 100,000 people. He had made countless TV appearances, been in over thirty films, and officially represented his country on three foreign continents. Always traveling with a typewriter, he had written two autobiographies. He was the first black man to have a national radio show.

Musically, he wrote dozens of songs and put many others on the map. He transformed singing by being the first to sing songs as freely as a jazz instrumentalist would play them. He would still sing the lyrics (mostly), but alter the rhythm and change the tune. He was improvising, in other words, and no one on record had sung like that before. Tony Bennett believes

> Armstrong practically invented jazz singing and was the greatest influence not only in jazz, but for all music. . . . Armstrong influ-

enced Billie Holiday, Sinatra, everybody. To this day in the music business . . . you'll find Armstrong got there first.

Bing Crosby said, "Do you realize that the greatest pop singer that ever was and ever will be forever and ever is Louis Armstrong?"

In addition to singing lyrics more freely, he pioneered "scat singing": eliminating the lyrics altogether and singing nonsense syllables. Imitating a horn, in other words. It's a staple of jazz singing now, made famous by greats like Ella Fitzgerald and Mel Tormé. Louis wasn't quite the first to do it on record, though he might have been the first to do it in an improvised (spur-of-the-moment) way. Regardless, he put scat singing on the map with one huge hit record that even changed how people spoke in Chicago.

If this weren't enough, Louis Armstrong changed how the trumpet was played, exploring with his high notes where no trumpeter had gone before. Early on, both jazz and classical players liked to examine his horn, expecting to find a trick trumpet. Each time, they discovered the magic was not in the horn, but in the man. Dizzy Gillespie, who took trumpeting to even greater heights in the 1940s and '50s said simply, "Without him, no me." Trumpeter Miles Davis pioneered several distinct styles of jazz and remarked, "You can't play anything on a horn that Louis hasn't played."

One last thing: in the 1920s he merely changed what jazz essentially was and established what it then would be. As a soloist in others' bands, he set the bar both for virtuosity and a relaxed, swinging feel. Then with the records he made with his own small combos, he established jazz as a music for soloists rather than the more collaborative, ensemble style it was before. Instead of B.C. and A.D., it wouldn't be at all unreasonable to date music history B.A. and A.A., if you know what I mean.

Jazz founder. Trumpet virtuoso. Pioneering vocalist. Jazz/pop crossover artist. Radio, movie, and TV star. Musical ambassador. International icon. And most importantly, a man who lived with the purpose of bringing joy to others and leaving the world better than he found it. His purpose and way of living are much harder to quantify than accolades and achievements, but ultimately far more important. As Duke Ellington put it, Louis was "born poor, died rich, and never hurt anyone along the way." As an educator, I'm not going to end up with one of my lesson plans onboard a spacecraft or be nominated to the Teaching Hall of Fame. I can, however, learn from the way Louis lived and be a better human being through his example. So in the pages to come, we'll explore ten aspects of living well, such as encouraging others, building on your strengths, showing courage, and living out a sense of purpose.

As we begin the first chapter, keep in mind Louis's accomplishments and the positive way he lived his life. Because now we're traveling back to the beginning, to appreciate the magnitude of the journey Louis Armstrong took. The man who died beloved by millions was born in a battlefield.

Listening Suggestions

Links to audio and video files are found at
www.livelikelouis.com.

Let's save trumpet virtuosity and scat singing for other chapters and focus here on how Louis improvised. That is, how he spontaneously created new tunes and rhythms.

It's impossible to hear Louis Armstrong now as people heard him in the 1920s and '30s when he was musically going where no "cat" had gone before. It's hard to hear how he's altering a tune or rhythm if we're not familiar with the "straight" (normal) version. Granted, the "standard" songs recorded by many artists over the years have had a resurgence lately, thanks to artists like Rod Stewart, Carly Simon, and Michael Bublé. Still, we're often unaware of the straight versions of Louis's songs, to appreciate how masterfully he changed them.

Of the songs Louis recorded in his most energetic years, "Georgia on My Mind" probably has the best chance of being known by us post-moderns, thanks to Ray Charles. Satchmo begins with eight measures played pretty straight; but he's already altering things a bit in the next eight bars. Sixteen measures of violins and syrupy saxes bring us to Louis's vocal treatment of the song. Listen to a masterful singer improvise, altering the song's tune and rhythm, though the melody is still close by. Then listen to the then-unequalled master of the trumpet improvise on his horn.

During his trumpet solo he'll even throw in a two-measure quote from "Rhapsody in Blue" for you, if you know that piece. Louis established jazz as a soloist's art and was the first player in modern times to show how improvisers could be just as beautifully imaginative as composers who write down their notes. In fact, jazz artists are composing a new melody each time they solo – and in front of an audience. No pressure there, eh?

There's another song by Hoagie Carmichael many of us still might know. It's "Stardust," of which *Wikipedia* presently says there are 1,800 recordings. Listen to Louis's 1931 recording. Most jazz artists will play a melody pretty straight the first time, with minimal changes. But right out of the blocks, King Louis is wonderfully altering an already-beautiful melody, though it's still recognizable. After he plays one chorus, he enters singing the same note repeatedly. Then he takes off. Groundbreaking. And just as important, joyful.

1   Don't Fence Me In

*in which Louis shows us
we can rise above our circumstances*

It wasn't just any battlefield Louis was born in, it was "The Battlefield," a poor black neighborhood in turn-of-the-century New Orleans. Try to imagine it in 1906: houses are closely packed, with outhouses in the back. Horses fill the streets, and the humid air is heavy with odors. The cries of street vendors are heard. The children are barefoot. One of them, a five-year-old boy, is returning from a cistern. He carries water for his caretaker grandmother. But when he arrives back at her small house, a mysterious old woman is with her; both wear serious expressions. The stranger says the boy is to leave the only home he has known and go with her. He must care for his sick mother.

His grandmother dresses him in the better of his two sets of clothing. "I really hate to let you out of my sight," she sighs. But as Louis would write in his memoirs five decades later, his grandmother is a "grand person" and doesn't think twice about parting with the boy so that his mother could be cared for. His touching reply, recollected fifty years later, shows how he treasured his grandmother:

> I am sorry to leave you too Granny. . . .You have been so kind and so nice to me, taught me everything I know: how to take care of myself, how to wash myself and brush my teeth, put my clothes away, mind the older folks.

Then his hand is taken by the stranger and he is led away. When they turn the corner and he can no longer see his grandmother, the boy naturally starts to cry. They wait for the trolley, in front of the House of Detention. The woman tells the five-year-old she'll have him sent there if he doesn't stop bawling. He takes her at her word. The streetcar arrives and, never having ridden one, the boy goes right to the front to get a good view. But this is 1906 in New Orleans, the city where Homer Plessy sued all the way to the Supreme Court to get railway cars desegregated. And lost. "Separate but equal" is the law of the land, and the boy cannot read the very large sign specifying where not to sit. The thrill of being on a streetcar has overcome his sorrow for a time and he is "acting cute" in the front.

The woman motions to the boy to come to the back of the trolley. He ignores her. She storms up and drags the "little fool" to the back. They ride for several minutes to the Back o' Town neighborhood near Liberty and Perdido streets, then walk two blocks to a room facing a back courtyard. There they find a very sick twenty-year-old woman on a pallet. It is Louis's mother and it is now his job to take care of her.

Louis's Upbringing

This key moment in Louis's life illustrates his child-hood and what he overcame. It is also very telling about his adult life, because what we know of this episode comes from recollections written in his fif-ties. The gratitude he expresses to his grandmother in his 1954 memoir exemplifies the gratitude he generally expressed throughout his life for a great many people and things, even events in his child-hood most would consider bad. Also, the event on the trolley shows him literally crossing the bound-ary between white and black. Later he would be the first black star embraced by whites, who would come to enjoy him more than fellow blacks did. Nevertheless, dealing with racism was a fact of life for any black man, whether entertainer or brick-layer. We'll explore these themes in later chapters. Let's examine Louis's childhood circumstances a bit more.

He was born to a fifteen-year-old mother and twenty-year-old father who weren't married and had an on-and-off sort of relationship. His mother gave birth in 1901 in his grandmother's house in the aforementioned "Battlefield" neighborhood of New Orleans. It was named the Battlefield because – why else? – it was the scene of considerable chaos and fighting. In fact, it was the black red-light district. Young Louis's neighbors were gamblers, thieves, pimps, and prostitutes, with some ordinary working stiffs mixed in: Louis's father worked at a turpentine factory until his death in 1933. But his parents split up shortly after his birth and both moved out after he was born, leaving him with his grandmother. Louis occasionally would see his father marching in parades, and would later write of the pride he had for the man and his skills in strutting. But aside from a brief stay with him as a teen, Louis had no real relationship with his father.

Louis's mother, Mayann, did indeed get well after he arrived to take care of her. Louis had a number of "stepfathers" (his mother's live-in boyfriends) who varied in their treatment of Mayann, Louis, and his little sister. Satchmo's biographers believe that at least occasionally Mayann prostituted herself, which would not have been uncommon for a single woman with children to support. Louis went to school though he was always working too, selling papers. He dropped out of the fifth grade when he was eleven years old and began singing for coins in a street quartet. (If you're ever at the Superdome, cross Poydras Street at Freret, and you can hang out on the corner where Pops first performed.) Like other boys attracted to illicit goings-on, he would linger outside rough honky-tonks like the "Funky Butt," peeking through cracks in the boards; or sneak into "Dago Tony's" and hide behind the piano to be near the musicians.

Then on New Year's Eve, 1912, Louis Armstrong fired a gun in the air and was sent to a reformatory, the Colored Waif's Home. After a year and a half, Louis was reluctant to leave that disciplined environment but was released nevertheless. He ended up with his father's second family for a time. Due to sibling troubles and his father's inability to provide, however, he returned to his mother and sister and helped support them, staying with them until leaving home in 1919. His mother took in laundry, they had no bathroom, and all shared one bed. Louis described the family as poor but "clean," and remarked in his 1954 memoir that all types of people treated Mayann with respect, and she in turn "always held her head up."

Louis then worked on a wagon delivering coal to prostitutes in Storyville, New Orleans' storied red-light district. On Saturday mornings he could sell buckets of brick dust to the working women there. They thought it good luck to sprinkle it on the walk after scrubbing the front steps with their urine. I can't attest to whether it actually brought them luck, but it stands as an example of what young Louis saw while growing up.

If we translated this to the twenty-first century, we really wouldn't have to change many of the details. A son with an absent father drops out of school, takes to the streets, commits a crime, does some time, gets out. What comes next? More jail time, right? After an initial lock up, it's likely in and out of jail or prison. There is little to show when death comes, probably at a young age through violence or substance abuse. I witnessed this pattern firsthand in a cheerful student of mine after he did time in a nearby juvenile lockup for stealing a van. He returned a different person, sullen, tough, and thinking himself a criminal. Having a rusted gun in his locker got him expelled, and so the cycle continued.

Future offenses and incarceration would be an accurate prediction in a lot of cases. But not always. And not in Louis's case. Remember his lifetime accomplishments? Plus all the joy he brought to his listeners? Clearly his rugged surroundings and early experiences did not define or confine him.

No Victim of Circumstances

Another star of the 1930s, Mr. Jerome Howard, used a certain line in many of his short films. He'd be surrounded by plumbing, or have a lobster stuck to his nose, with his brother about to slap him. Wanting to escape the inevitable, he'd plead, "I'm just a victim of 'coicumstance'!" You might know Jerome better by his stage name, Curly, of the Three Stooges. And if you've seen a Stooges film, I'm sure you can hear his high-pitched voice making that claim (probably followed by a couple of "nyuk-nyuks" and the slap from Moe).

Unlike Curly, however, Louis Armstrong – though raised in abject poverty and surrounded by crime and substance abuse – never claimed to be a victim of circumstance. His very challenging circumstances did not define him, just as your circumstances do not have to define you; neither the situation when you were young nor your situation now. This is an old truth, as most truths are. But it bears hearing again.

Certainly, Louis's circumstances did influence

him. This is inescapable. We're always being influenced by everything around us. Some fascinating research placed people in a room where the Apple Computer logo was subtly displayed; others were in a room with the IBM logo. Which people performed more creatively? I don't even have to tell you, do I? We've been pummeled for years by ads telling us PC is boring and Mac is cool. Just their logos affected people's behavior without their even knowing. In a similar experiment, people were assigned to a room with either the Disney logo or the E Entertainment Network logo. One group responded to questions more truthfully. Guess which group. (Hint: it wasn't the group seeing the logo we associate with celebrity dirt and gossip.)

And if logos influence us, how much more so do *people*? Famous research by Solomon Asch in the 1950s placed one person among a group. Everyone else in the group was "in" on the experiment. These undercover participants would discuss three lines on a paper and come to a very wrong group decision on which two were the same length. Asch observed that when three others agreed on a wrong answer, the unknowing individual would often go along with that obviously wrong group statement, although he or she knew it to be false. And history shows us that even a whole nation can take a terrible wrong turn as neighbor reinforces neighbor in some horrific belief or attitude. We must acknowledge the strong pull exerted on us by the things and people in our surroundings. "Lie down with dogs, get up with fleas," some dog-hater once put it.

But whether, and for how long we lie down

with them, *is* at least somewhat up to us. And so is how we respond and react to the fleas. Not every participant agreed with the obviously wrong group decisions in Asch's conformity experiments. Not every German went along with Hitler; some were even executed for resisting the Nazis. And not everyone raised in crime and poverty succumbs to it. Otherwise Louis and others from such circumstances would never escape it as they certainly have. The pull of the things and people around us is strong, yes, but not irresistible.

This is not to deny the difficulty of circumstances you've been through or are facing right now. As we've seen, situations and the people around us can be very challenging and powerful. But odds are, if you've lived through difficulties, you can think right now of one way they helped make you a better person. Even in the case of abuse, a terrible thing. Most abusers were themselves abused as children, which shows the power of that very painful situation. But it is not all-powerful. The vast majority of abused people do not become abusers. Most do not let that situation define them; they go on to be good parents or spouses. In fact, such men and women often make a decided effort to be especially loving because of what was done to them. In Louis's case it's not a stretch to say that without his background his artistry would have turned out very differently. He played and sang from what he knew, and the world has never been the same.

The Armstrong biographies and Louis's own writings don't reveal him to have been extremely driven to escape poverty, as some people are. "I never did want to be a big mucky-muck star," he said. But escape poverty he did, to say the least. Until the day he left New Orleans to play in a riverboat orchestra, he was always working. Selling papers and working on a junk wagon as a child. Then working on coal carts, in coal yards, and on the docks unloading banana boats as a teen. And all the while practicing his cornet (a horn slightly rounder than a trumpet) and playing in bands whenever he could. So although it doesn't seem he was consciously striving to escape poverty, his attitude insured – as much as anything can – that he would not be a victim of it.

Poverty or any of a hundred other challenging conditions such as illness, difficult neighbors, or an abusive boss, are very serious, powerful things. I'm careful in choosing my words, though. I'm hesitant to label circumstances or events as "bad," because I've known people who became as positive or successful as they are *due to* the challenging events. Composer Wayne Shorter writes that "noble human behavior may remain dormant unless 'awakened' due to trials and tribulations." Perhaps something that seemed bad at one point in your life can even be seen as a blessing now when you look back on it.

A friend of mine had to have brain surgery. That's bad, right? Except it saved her life. That's good. The surgeon nicked a nerve that controls some facial muscles. Now my friend can't open her eye, although the eye itself still works. That's a bad thing, right? Can't you imagine someone being sad or bitter about that for the rest of her life? But a bit after the operation, she actually said she was glad it happened. You see, I misled you a bit; she can open the eye by hand. And she does so . . . when looking through a telescope. She's an amateur astronomer. A stargazer can see especially well with an eye that's been closed for days, making it very dilated and ready to take in a stunning amount of starlight.

Likewise, in a recent commercial, Michael J. Fox reports that Parkinson's has given him something to be thankful for: the ability to make a difference. Contemporary spiritual teachers Dr. Depak Chopra and Ekhart Tolle both routinely make the point that the externals of our world are really things that we interpret, and it is actually these perceptions that form the "world" each of us lives in mentally. Dr. Chopra writes, "Every situation is a choice in consciousness, and a recognition of that choice as the outer world." As bad as many of us would consider young Louis's circumstances, he did not see them that way. In fact he always spoke fondly of his childhood days and the characters he grew up around. "Every time I close my eyes blowing that trumpet of mine — I look right in the heart of good old New Orleans. . . . It has given me something to live for."

"But I'm not from poverty."

If you're not from poverty or such immediately challenging circumstances, you still might have an environment or background that can hold you back, even being from the middle class. In the documentary "Buena Vista Social Club," a film about the fantastic musical world of Cuba, there's a moment where an old Cuban says, "If we had followed the way of possessions, we would have disappeared long ago." He reminds me of the Buddha, who taught how craving leads to disappointment and suffering; and of Jesus, who said, "Your life does not consist of your possessions." Certainly Cuba has serious problems, but it also has far more dancing and live music than you find here in the United States. It's everywhere in Cuba. In fact, if you watch and listen to that film, it's hard to argue that Cuba doesn't have, well, more *soul* than America does. Gerry Goffin and Carol King wrote for the Monkees back in 1967 that creature comfort goals tend to numb our souls and make it hard for us to see.

No, I'm not advocating for the Amish life as I sit writing this book on a laptop (although some research does show the Amish being slightly happier than the general public). I'm merely trying to say that a relatively good life economically can have negative effects on someone just as rough circumstances can. We all know of wealthy children spoiled by their cushy circumstances just as a poor child can be stunted by poverty. Andrew Carnegie, a firsthand expert on wealth, actually said, "The richest heritage a man can have is to be born into poverty."

Yet many people from the upper class do go on to be of service to others. A good number of the Progressive Era's reformers were from wealthy families, as were the Roosevelts and Kennedys. Many have used their wealth to build businesses, fund community institutions, even eradicate diseases. These people's comfortable circumstances didn't define them and make them spoiled slugs, just as Louis's background didn't make him feel like a victim and stay stuck in poverty.

You're probably not one of the wealthy "One Percent," I know. But very possibly, you did have a relatively decent upbringing with abundant material goods, especially compared with much of the world. And decent circumstances when young might have led you to be living on achievement-drive or consumerism-autopilot now. Our culture certainly encourages it. How many commercial images are you bombarded with per day? Life is presented as being all about owning the new thing and looking right. Even our government of the people, by the people, and for the people refers to us as "consumers." But comfortable circumstances do not have to define us, numbing our souls, making us mindless consumer sheep. Even if you were a kid from a decent family (maybe even, like me, from the suburbs – a double whammy), you can still find some cause or higher purpose that gives your life meaning and helps other people too.

A contractor, rather than just earning his daily bread, can consciously give people the best roof or basement possible, to help them be warm and dry for a long time.

A businesswoman, rather than just enjoying the game and making some money, can be involved in a company that really benefits people and can focus on helping others.

A police officer, rather than just working a shift

and getting home, can be committed to justice and protecting people.

A teacher, rather than just doing a job to feed his kids and help them through college, can commit himself to a higher goal of helping young people become more intelligent and responsible.

A parent, rather than just surviving another day with only two more gray hairs, can consciously work at raising the best human beings possible. God knows we need as many compassionate, proactive people as we can get.

I don't mean to assume you're *not* living for a higher goal. But I know how it goes: I am sometimes that teacher two paragraphs up. I know in my head that there are higher goals to pursue, but I'm often stuck for days on autopilot, performing a "day job." I merely offer the above contrasts as reminders, in case you too have been stuck on autopilot lately. We will have more to discuss about purpose near the end of the book. But for now, suffice it to say that the drudgery of daily life or the tyranny of the urgent do not have to dictate who we are or what we live for.

I am aware that saying middle class people can be handicapped in their own way might be insulting to those who come from poverty. Truly, I mean no offense; the point is just that each of us has circumstances that can limit us somehow. What is clear is that Louis did not let his circumstances limit who he was. He followed his inspiration to make music, worked very hard at it, and led a meaningful life. Instead of giving in to a very rough environment, he took what he saw and experienced, and played it back out to the world through his music.

True, you're not a great trumpet player born at the turn of the century. However, you *can* live like Louis: you can rise above your circumstances to daily create a life of purpose and fulfillment. May you meet with success and joy in that endeavor!

Practices

Some people believe there is a personal God or gods in control of things. Others believe in an intelligence or spirit pervading all things. If you hold to either of these paradigms, it can be helpful to give thanks to God or the universe for bringing you into tough circumstances or for bringing difficult people into your life. And even if you don't believe in any overarching power that might have brought you into tough times, you can still express gratitude for those circumstances.

Giving thanks for difficulties might sound odd. However, when we give thanks, we just plain feel better. It is an old cliché, but adopting an "attitude of gratitude" can work wonders in you and then through you.

Our logical, Western minds might still need a reason to give thanks for difficulties. Why give thanks for tough conditions? Try reflecting on what the circumstances taught you about yourself. Maybe you didn't handle them so well (I'm thinking of some specific times in *my* life right now, by the way). This can teach you where you might yet need to grow. Knowing yourself better is very valuable and worth giving thanks for.

Also, you can examine yourself and see how you *have* grown because of the difficulties. Louis certainly became the artist he was, partly due to his surroundings and experiences.

You might try copying and finishing these sentences in a notebook:

I am actually thankful for . . . [name a difficulty or challenge].

How I handled it teaches me about myself that I . . .

It helped me grow because . . .

We're a short-attention-span culture, trained to move quickly from one thing to the next. But if you will write the above sentences several times, over several days, they can be effective. They can help change your thoughts and feelings about the past, thus actually changing the interior world you live in. And as you grow in self-understanding, this in turn can help you be of more benefit to others. Like Louis, you can rise above difficult circumstances and even use them to bless other people.

Listening Suggestions

Links to audio and video files are found at
www.livelikelouis.com.

Despite his challenging environment during child-
hood and the racism of the Jim Crow South, Louis
made several records singing about a romanticized,
mythical Dixie. These include his theme song,
"When It's Sleepy Time Down South." The original
1931 version opens with some dialog between Louis
and his pianist who have met in the North and long
to go back home to eat some red beans and rice –
Louis's favorite food. This version has "darkies"
and "mammy" in it, but if you can accept these
words as being of their time, you'll hear Pops sing
in a very heartfelt manner. A later example of this
nostalgic style of song is "Do You Know What It
Means to Miss New Orleans?"

2 *Keep the Rhythm Going*

*in which Louis's mentors remind us
of the importance of encouragement*

"Louis Armstrong, how would you like to join our brass band?" This simple question was asked by the music instructor at a boys' reformatory in 1913. His eleven words changed the course not just of a life, but of American popular music. And it was all because a young instructor saw some good in a "bad" kid and decided to nurture his potential. That teacher, Peter Davis, along with Louis's later musical mentor, Joe Oliver, remind us of the importance of encouragement.

But how did Louis end up in New Orleans' Colored Waif's Home? If you recall, young Louis decided to fire off a gun on New Year's Eve, 1912. "Decided" is probably too strong a word to describe the actions of an eleven and a half year old boy, however. Knowing New Orleans' rowdy holiday traditions, Louis had swiped a pistol from one of his "stepfathers" and tucked it in his shirt. He and his quartet were out walking Rampart Street, singing for pennies when they heard someone across the street celebrating with a gun. His buddies yelled to Louis, "Go get him, Dipper!" So "Dippermouth" Armstrong obliged, impulsively firing his gun into the air. Writing about the incident decades later, Satchmo triumphantly recalled that his was the better, noisier gun and the other kid quickly took off.

Louis got away with firing his gun. Once. But the second time he fired shots into the air, it turned into a not-so-happy new year. His arms were immediately gripped tight from behind. A detective had been watching. Despite Louis's pleas to be sent home, the detective arrested the boy. Apparently the justice system moved a bit quicker back then: the very next day he was sentenced to the Colored Waif's Home, a military style reformatory five miles away from Louis's neighborhood. It might as well have been five hundred. The Home was surrounded by farms and gardens. Instead of hearing "King" Oliver's cornet belting out from a nearby honkeytonk, Louis now fell asleep to the sounds of nearby cattle and awoke with the chickens. It was one of the best things that ever happened to him.

Captain Jones, the superintendent, was strict but fair. The one hundred or so boys were awakened by bugle and practiced military drills in the yard. There was work to do every day, while the food and sleeping arrangements were spartan but adequate. The boys had to keep themselves and the Home clean. All learned trade skills. Some learned music.

Armstrong experts and Louis's own accounts differ as to when he first picked up a cornet (that slightly mellower version of the trumpet). He probably had a secondhand horn and was shown a few "licks" prior to his arrival at the Waif's Home. But without a doubt, the instruction he got at the Home from Mr. Davis was his first real musical training and his first experience in a band. But he almost didn't get that experience.

Mr. Davis didn't like him at first. Louis was a "bad" kid from a bad neighborhood. He hadn't just shoplifted or played truant, he had fired gunshots in public. But as the weeks went on, Mr. Davis softened. They say the child is father to the man, so it's easy to imagine Louis being very personable even at eleven. Mr. Davis would occasionally make eye contact with him and give a little smile. Since Louis had been abandoned by his own father, just a smile from the man made him "feel good inside." Occasionally Davis would speak to the boy. In 1954 Louis still vividly remembered how good even a little encouragement felt: "Gee, what a feeling, that coming from him!" Then after about six months, Davis approached Louis at supper and asked him that fateful question: Did he want to join the band? Louis was speechless. Mr. Davis had to repeat himself. Louis then happily accepted, washed up, and went to rehearsal. He was officially handed . . . a tambourine.

It wasn't exactly what he was hoping for. Cornet was the prestige instrument of the day, whether in a concert band like John Philip Sousa's or a little jazz combo back in the Third Ward of New Orleans. A gleaming, triumphant cornet, that's what Louis had been dreaming of playing. But it was not where a fellow began. Dues must be paid. So tambourine came first. Louis made the most of it and his perseverance paid off. "Mr. Davis nodded with approval which was all I needed. His approval was all important for any boy who wanted a musical career." Davis promoted Louis to alto horn. Louis continued to practice and earn Mr. Davis's approval.

Then a lucky break: the Home's bugler was released to his parents. Now was Louis's chance! Mr. Davis asked Louis to be the bugler. He polished the horn, practiced hard, and played well. His diligence and talent earned him the right to play cornet. Mr. Davis taught him "Home, Sweet Home," and Louis later recalled, "I was in seventh heaven. Unless I was dreaming, my ambition had been realized." I smile every time I read that remembrance, hearing in it a boy's happiness and pride.

After practicing diligently on cornet, Louis was approached by Mr. Davis: "Louis, I am going to make you leader of the band." The boy leapt up and whooped for joy right in front of his mentor. He would lead the band in its resplendent uniforms all throughout greater New Orleans. They played in the frequent parades for which the Crescent City is still famous, and at many picnics and social events. The boy was now a musician and a leader. The Louis Armstrong we know and love was on his way, thanks to the perception and encouragement of Mr. Peter Davis.

A King, but Not Too Proud to Be a Mentor

I mentioned "King" Oliver in passing, a few paragraphs back. By Louis's teen years, Joe Oliver was the top cornet player in the parade bands and jazz combos of New Orleans. As such, he took his place in a lineage of local cornet kings. Rival Bunk Johnson was giving Oliver a run for his money as top player, but Louis considered Joe Oliver the best. Louis wrote,

> The way I see it, the greatest musical creations came from his horn – and I've heard a lot of them play. . . . Joe Oliver *created* things. . . . When he played his cornet there were always happiness.

As local cornet master and star of the Onward Brass Band, Joe Oliver might simply have enjoyed his fame and moved onward and upward in the musical world. Instead he chose also to teach and encourage a young hanger-on who would eventually surpass his master. In 1960 Louis would write that Oliver "had a heart as big as a whale when it came to helping the underdog in music such as me. I was just a kid, Joe saw I had possibilities and he'd go out of his way to help me or any other ambitious kid who were interested in their instrument as I were."

When Joe was done with a parade, he'd let the teenage Louis carry his horn. Oliver later gave him an old cornet which Louis "guarded with his life." King Oliver was willing to show him "anything I wanted to know" on the horn. Moreover, Mrs. Oliver would have Louis run errands for her, often invited him to stay for supper, and in many ways treated him like a son. This adopted family made quite an impression, as Louis would later make clear in an unpublished memoir. "I shall never forget how Joe Oliver and his wife, Mrs. Stella Oliver, were so nice to me in New Orleans, when I was quite a youngster."

One story marvelously illustrates the interest Joe Oliver took in the young Louis Armstrong. Around 1917, Armstrong and a buddy put together their own combo. Bands would advertise upcoming appearances by playing while riding through the streets on a wagon. When competing bands would meet, they would have an impromptu "cutting" contest to determine who was better and drum up business. Oliver gave Louis a special signal: if their bands were to meet, Louis should stand up so Oliver would see him. Oliver's band would then play a couple of numbers to show who was boss, but not embarrass the youngsters too badly. Oliver's group would also pointedly omit a tune usually played as a comical dismissal of a vanquished band.

One time the wagons met and Louis forgot to stand up. Without that signal Oliver's band competed full force and demolished the boys. Oliver later gave Louis an earful for not signaling him to go easy on his young friend. Mentor and apprentice swiftly patched it up, however, over a bottle of beer. This was especially impressive to Louis since King Oliver was a bit tight with his money, at least in the drink-buying department. "But for me he would do anything," he wrote.

Oliver left New Orleans in 1918, part of the

Great Migration of Southern blacks to find freedom from Jim Crow and poverty. First he toured. Then he established King Oliver's Creole Jazz Band in 1922 and became ensconced at Chicago's famed Lincoln Gardens ballroom. He was the talk of that toddlin' town. And who took Oliver's place back in New Orleans? Louis Armstrong, of course. From his work in dance bands and his prominent role in the Tuxedo Brass Band, Louis's reputation grew and spread. "I could go into any part of New Orleans without being bothered. Everybody loved me and just wanted to hear me." With Louis obviously possessing serious talent, it might seem inevitable to us modern, mobile people that he too would leave New Orleans. But Louis was really a homebody. He loved his mother's red beans and rice, and he had seen too many friends leave home and meet with trouble. "I had made up my mind that I would not leave New Orleans unless the King sent for me."

The king beckoned.

Oliver's telegrams gave a young, home-loving, Southern black man the courage to board the Illinois Central line and leave everything he knew behind him, armed only with a valise, a cornet, and a fish sandwich lovingly packed by his mother. When he got off the train in Chicago, Stella and Joe Oliver fed him and made rooming arrangements. Louis played second cornet that night with his idol and father figure. At the end of the evening, Oliver even let the young man take a solo. They soon became famous for playing "breaks" in the music together in harmony. Usually in such breaks all the other musicians suddenly stop and let one soloist shine for a couple of measures. But Oliver shared the spotlight with Louis, the two of them displaying a musical affinity that became legendary.

A decision to tour broke up that great band. Louis and his wife, Lil, the group's piano player, were the only two who stayed with Oliver. After the tour, Oliver's Creole Jazz Band was no more. The King took a position in another group, and Louis got the call to go to New York, to the top black dance orchestra there. Oliver and Armstrong went their separate ways, professionally. But for the rest of his life, Louis would talk of how he felt about "Papa" Joe, who had taken the time to teach and encourage him: "I can never stop loving Joe Oliver. He was always ready to come to my rescue when I needed someone to tell me about life and its little intricate things, and help me out of difficult situations."

The Power of Encouragement

I freely acknowledge that I am not to teaching, parenting, or living, what Joe Oliver was to cornet playing. Nevertheless, there are plenty of people I come across in my life I can encourage in some way. The German poet Goethe wrote, "Correction does much, but encouragement does more." And education expert Linda Albert advises my fellow teachers and me, "Encouragement is the most powerful tool we possess." They couldn't be righter. Think back to people who encouraged you. I'll bet you remember their attitude. It was positive. They had confidence in you and it showed. The root of "courage," by the way, is the Latin word *cor*, or "heart." So the people who encouraged you spoke to your heart and gave you strength to face a challenge and believe in yourself.

Sometimes it seems we're drowning in words lately, especially if you browse through cable TV or talk radio. Encouragement, however, is one area where words *are* often necessary and can actually do some lasting good. Go to any youth sporting event and you'll hear how natural it is for parents to yell encouraging words to their children. Out on the soccer fields in my town, you're liable to hear parents yell things like "Stay with him, Brett," or "Good save, Liz." There's no instruction there, just words meant to fire the kid up a bit and help her performance. But does it really do any good?

A team of sports science researchers in Pennsylvania set out in 2002 to investigate that very question. They pre-tested a number of men and women on treadmill performance; then divided them into groups receiving either frequent, infrequent, or no words of encouragement during a second attempt. Comparing their pre- and post-tests, those who were encouraged more frequently (every 20 or 60 seconds) put forth "significantly greater maximum effort," felt less tired, and even had better oxygen usage. Just hearing words of encouragement does change how we feel and act.

That's scientific evidence from the laboratory. Here are some examples of words of encouragement recently overheard in real life:

Someone is having a hard time finding a job. Her friend commiserates but also adds, "Hang in there, the right job is out there somewhere."

A child is having a hard time with the challenge of helping clean a relative's vacant house. His dad says, "I have confidence in you," and compliments the boy's perseverance when he finishes the task.

A colleague is thinking about making a career change. His friend offers advice and adds, "But I know you'll be good at whichever one you pick."

A student is having a hard time choosing a topic for a demonstration speech. The teacher doesn't try to solve the problem for her; instead she asks several questions to guide her, then says, "I'm sure you'll choose a good topic." (She eventually picked a great topic, by the way: a magic trick that still stumps those of us who missed her speech!)

A lot in our culture seems set up to promote and benefit from strife and nastiness. Sharing encouragement is one easy way to counter that trend and give the universe a gentle nudge back in the direction of kindness and cooperation. As bandleader Stan Kenton put it, "When you get to the top, don't forget to send the elevator down for the next guy." Hearing about the encouragers in Louis's life and remembering those recent examples from my own experience motivate me to want to do likewise. Maybe it will be just through a few words of hope to someone at home or at work; maybe through a more purposeful mentoring relationship. Whatever your situation, you too can be like Peter Davis and King Oliver. You can encourage a friend or co-worker to grow or take a chance or keep on going during a tough time. You probably won't make someone the next cornet king. But you *will* make a difference.

Practices

Every morning for a week, before you start your day, try thinking of someone who has encouraged you. Recollect what words he or she said to cheer or hearten you, and how the words were delivered. Bring to mind how the encourager's attitude empowered you and made you feel. Then write the person's name on a piece of paper and put it in your pocket; or on a sticky note placed where you'll see it during your day. Each time you notice it, say to yourself,

"Be like _____ today."

To take it a step further, bring to mind the people you generally interact with and see if anyone seems particularly in need of encouragement. Resolve to find a way to cheer or strengthen that person today. Plan the words in advance, or leave it to the moment, but seek him or her out and be an encourager. Remember the effect that Peter Davis and Joe Oliver had on Louis. When you change how one person feels or acts, you have changed the world.

Listening Suggestions

Links to audio and video files are found at
www.livelikelouis.com.

"Snake Rag," by King Oliver's Creole Jazz Band in 1923, is a fun, comical piece. You can hear Louis and King Oliver taking their famous breaks together when everything in the music stops but them. You also get a good example of polyphonic music, the essence of early jazz. Literally it means "many sounds," which refers to the wind instruments all playing seemingly independent lines at the same time, yet meshing together gloriously.

"Chimes Blues," recorded the day before, is the King Oliver piece Ken Burns selected for his terrific CD anthology of Louis's music. Again, there is wonderful polyphonic playing, plus you can hear the future Mrs. Armstrong simulating chimes. You'll hear an extended solo about two minutes into the record: it's Satchmo's first recorded solo. Writer and Armstrong scholar Gary Giddins says when you hear it you're hearing the future.

Finally, on this book's companion website you'll find links to two segments from the old TV show *I've Got a Secret*. I heartily recommend viewing them. I won't reveal the secret, but the ending is one of the most touching things I've ever seen.

3   I Get Ideas

*in which Louis reminds us
of the value of an open mind*

Over the years, a number of keen-eyed observers
have noticed that in some photographs you can
spot Pops wearing a small medallion. This particular piece of jewelry has piqued people's curiosity
enough that there's even a question and answer
thread about it on the *Yahoo!Answers* website. The
interest is because the medallion Louis wore relig-
iously in his later years was a Star of David. Why
would Louis Armstrong, a black man baptized
Catholic in New Orleans, wear the symbol of Juda-
ism? The answer lies in a family's kindness to him,
and in Louis's openness to a wide variety of ideas.

One of the most important factors in Louis's ris-
ing above poverty and a crime-saturated neighborhood was how people nurtured and looked out for
him. We've already met his mother, Peter Davis,
and the Olivers. In addition to them, Louis was
sheltered and looked-after by the Karnofskys, a
Jewish family he worked for as a boy. They were a
family of peddlers who had come from Lithuania,

and their generous treatment of one child would pay huge dividends for American music. Little Louis assisted in buying up rags, bones, and other junk. He also rode along on their wagon to help the Karnofskys sell coal to prostitutes in New Orleans' Storyville red-light district. To advertise their business in the age before television commercials and internet pop-up ads, the two Karnofsky brothers employed Louis to blow on a tin horn to announce their wagon's approach. One day the wagon passed a pawn shop; from behind the window, an old cornet grabbed Louis's attention. It was priced at five dollars, though, far more than the boy had. To help Louis buy the instrument, Morris Karnofsky advanced him two dollars. Louis paid the rest in fifty-cent installments out of his pay.

Perhaps as important as lending Louis the money for a horn, the Karnofskys were also very encouraging. "The Karnofsky family kept reminding me that I had talent," Louis wrote.

> Although I could not play a good tune Morris applauded me just the same, which made me feel very good. As a young boy coming up, the people whom I worked for were very much concerned about my future in music. They could see that I had music in my soul. They really wanted me to be something in life. And music was it. Appreciating my every effort.

In this recollection written in his late sixties, you can't miss hearing the fondness Louis Armstrong still felt for that family. The Karnofskys were whites who dared treat a black child like one of the family. After a day of junk peddling and an evening of selling coal, they would feed him, leading to his life-long affinity for matzos. Before sending Louis home for the night, the Karnofskys would let him partici-pate in a family ritual as they sang the baby to sleep. "They were always warm and kind to me, which was very noticeable to me – just a kid who could use a little word of kindness, something that a kid could use at seven, and just starting out in the world." Their kind treatment greatly affected Louis: "I will love the Jewish people all of my life," he wrote near the end of it.

As to the Star of David necklace itself, it was given to Louis by his longtime manager, Joe Glaser, who was Jewish. The mid-1930s was a low period in Pops' career. Glaser helped Louis sort out his busi-ness affairs, resolving a potentially lethal conflict between two mob-connected agents both claiming Satchmo as their own. Also, the contract he secured for Louis with Decca Records greatly expanded Satchmo's popularity. For more than thirty years, Glaser would oversee Louis's career, helping him reach countless people and become an American icon. Louis had planned to publish his memories of the Karnofskys and he dedicated the work to Glaser, "The best Friend / That I've ever had / May the Lord Bless Him / Watch over him always." Be-cause of the Karnofskys' care and Glaser's attentive management, Louis Armstrong, a black son of the South, felt warmly toward the Jewish people all his life.

Cats of Any Color

Louis was also open-minded about race. "He was the least prejudiced musician I ever knew," recalled photographer George Schnitzer. This is not to say he was ignorant of his country's racial problems. That was impossible. In fact, one of his most famous quips came after a friend asked him what was new. Louis's reply: "Nothin' new. White folks still ahead." And we'll read in chapter eight how Louis jeopardized his career with some deliberately blunt comments about discrimination in the 1950s. But although he was very aware of racism, he was open-minded when it came to people and their race. "White audiences from all over the world picked up on my music, from the first note that I ever blown. And until these days they are still with me," he wrote in 1969. He spoke glowingly of the other great jazz trumpeter of the Roaring Twenties, the German-descended Bix Beiderbecke: "Those pretty notes went right through me."

Moreover, Louis made one of the first jazz records with a racially mixed group. On that record date, Pops was very moved by the playing of white trombonist (and future close friend) Jack Teagarden. Louis ascended a stepladder and sat up near a skylight to absorb Teagarden's beautiful sounds as he warmed up. The recording engineer had to invite Louis back down to make the record. Describing the white trombonist's musicality, Louis placed his hand over his heart, saying, "It moves me, it moves me right through here."

In 1947, as the swing band era was ending,

Louis put together a great small group he called the All Stars. Though the personnel would change over the next two decades, this would be the group he played and toured with relentlessly for the rest of his days. Right from the start it was racially mixed; and there at the beginning was a white man who was about as close to a peer as Louis had: trombone virtuoso Jack Teagarden, whom Louis had ascended the stepladder to hear in 1929. Louis declared, "Those people who make the restrictions, they don't know nothing about music, it's no crime for cats of any color to get together and blow."

On tour in the Middle East in 1959, Pops played in both Lebanon and Israel. In each country he was challenged by reporters, for making music for the Other. "Let me tell you something, man. That horn, you see that horn? That horn ain't prejudiced. A note's a note in any language."

Eclectic Musical Tastes

In the late 1930s, jazz aficionados were critical of Louis for abandoning the "pure" jazz of his records of the 1920s. He was now recording pop tunes with a larger band backing his playing and singing. But the critics were ignoring the full output of his earlier recordings, many of which featured singing, talking, even comedy. Louis never considered himself purely a jazz player; he was an overall musician and entertainer. First on the riverboats, then in Chicago, Louis played in orchestras that performed all kinds of music, from waltzes to polkas to light classics to "hot" jazz. This served to broaden his already wide-ranging taste in music. Louis's early record collection included opera star Enrico Caruso and Irish tenor John McCormack. Biographer Terry Teachout believes their expressive style helped influence Pops' soaring, expansive trumpet solos.

Louis's broad taste in music was reflected in various ways. He recorded with country music pioneer Jimmie Rodgers in 1930 and with Johnny Cash in 1970. Late in life he made a whole album of country songs and one entirely of Disney tunes. He died with over 600 reels of tape onto which he had transferred much of his 1200-item record collection of classics, opera, pop, Broadway, and modern jazz. In 1968 Louis listed Barbara Streisand's "People" as a record he'd take to a desert island. He praised the Beatles, describing them as "right outa the old spirituals and soul and country music and jazz." His favorite music other than his own was the Guy Lombardo band. Though most jazz fans found Lombardo's Royal Canadians "syrupy" or "corny," Louis liked their danceable beat and the fact that they never strayed far from a song's melody. Judging one of Lombardo's tunes once, Pops exclaimed, "Give this son of a gun *eight* stars! Lombardo!" Satchmo's taste in music was nothing if not wide-ranging.

The Value of Openness

Being open to many different styles of music is an example of a cluster of similar personality traits discovered by researchers. Using math to analyze thousands of personality tests given in the 20th century, psychologists found that many specific personality traits are linked together. For instance, individuals who are very "orderly" also tend to be very "precise" and "punctual." And people low in one tend to be low in the other two. Such similarities have led behavioral scientists to recognize five major clusters of personality traits they call the Big Five. One such mega-trait is Openness to Experience. And if anyone ever would have scored high in Openness, it was Louis Armstrong.

"Openness to Experience" sounds at first hearing as if it should be about bungee jumping or scuba diving, and indeed it could include these. But psychologists view Openness as being more about interests in diverse areas, being imaginative, and being intellectually and artistically curious. Of course, some people aren't like that at all, and that's no sin or crime. Rating low in this trait doesn't make someone a bad person. Like many traits, we need people at both ends of the spectrum, and when it comes to Openness, we need some meat-n-potatoes, normalcy-is-good folks, for sure. Just as we need the folks at the other end, like Louis. Once, when learning about the jazz age in U.S. History class, I and my students looked at some pretty far-out paintings by artists of the Harlem Renaissance. Some students responded by proclaiming the works weird, while others thought them interesting or cool. (And of course, there were plenty of kids in the middle.)

Research with identical twins reared apart has

shown that about fifty percent of the differences among us in any given trait is due to our genes. Someone born to real meat-n-potatoes parents will probably never become a wide-open urban hipster, and that's fine. But fifty percent from DNA still leaves about half our personality resulting from our upbringing and environment. So we're not fated through our genes to turn out exactly a certain way in any trait. Rather, it seems we're born with a set "range." Where we end up within that range is affected by our environment. And that environment includes much over which we have control.

Through what we read, view, and listen to, and by the people we hang out with, we can end up reinforcing our own likes and preferences. This is natural, but treading the same path over and over can turn it into a rut. On the other hand, we can stretch and experience things outside our proverbial comfort zones. Being open to new ideas might even help you live a longer, more productive life. Scientists have known for a while that simply keeping the brain active, even just by doing crosswords, can delay the onset of Alzheimer's disease. Now, recent research shows that learning a new language is especially helpful in delaying the course of that disorder. Of course aside from biological benefits, searching out new ideas or perspectives can help you grow in other ways.

Here I should mention the book you now hold (or read on your tablet device) came about from a little out-of-the-comfort-zone serendipity. While walking past the "new books" section at my local Mind and Soul Center (the public library), I spied a paperback titled *Me 2.0* in the business section, not one of my usual haunts. But after looking it over, I was intrigued, took it home (after checking it out, of course) and entered the world of "personal branding" under the guidance of author and consultant Dan Schawbel. In his book, he recommends "writing your book" as if doing so is a matter of course, something anyone can and should do. So, thanks to a book I wouldn't ordinarily find myself reading, inspiration struck, hard-but-enjoyable work began, and this book was created. It makes you wonder what other adventures might be in store, through future wandering away from the comfortable.

Recommending an excursion away from the familiar is not to say you shouldn't deeply hold some beliefs or outlooks, or enjoy one type of art or magazine or even person over another. To paraphrase a country song, you have to stand for something or you'll fall for anything. But we can hold our beliefs and enjoy what we enjoy without insulting or belittling others of a different opinion, as some people feel the need to do. And, by considering other positions or approaches, we'll remember that the people who hold differing viewpoints are just as smart and worthwhile as we are, no matter how loudly some pundit might tell us otherwise.

Louis Armstrong's love of the Jewish people, his acceptance of whites in an overtly racist age, and his broad taste in music remind us of the value of openness. Even if you were born to be essentially a meat-n-potatoes person, you might try a different cut of meat or swap in a new side dish every now and then. Prepare to be pleasantly surprised!

Practices

Option A, food:
Let's begin with the meat-n-potatoes metaphor and take it literally. Buy at the store, or sample at a restaurant, a food you've never had before. Even if you end up not caring for it, try to imagine why some people find it enjoyable. And if you do like it, give thanks for a new pleasure in life.

Option B, politics:
Read an article by a reasonable spokesperson of a viewpoint different from yours. Stay far away from extreme blowhards of any political persuasion unless you need a laugh. If you're more liberal, try reading David Frum; if you're more conservative, Robert Reich. Listen for the underlying assumptions that are different from yours, and why they might make sense to other people. One website that has reasonable arguments from both sides is *The Moderate Voice* at www.themoderatevoice.com.

Option C, music:
Deliberately listen to some music you ordinarily wouldn't. A student just had me listen to some Justin Bieber a couple of days ago, and you know what? It wasn't bad. It was fun and listenable, certainly no worse than a lot of other things I've heard.

Currently the iTunes store has a free single of the week and a "discovery download" featuring a different genre each week. Try to hear the good in what you choose, and consider why it appeals to its fans. Dancing, as always, remains an option.

Listening Suggestions

Links to audio and video files are found at
www.livelikelouis.com.

The fun "Knockin' a Jug" is the record made in 1929 after Louis came down off his stepladder to play with trombone genius Jack Teagarden. Teagarden is the first soloist, and you can hear why Louis was so knocked out.

In 1930 Louis performed on "Blue Yodel #9" by the early country artist Jimmie Rodgers. You can fast forward forty years and experience the same piece in a televised duet with Johnny Cash.

We'll have much more to say about the haunting "Black and Blue" in chapter eight. But for now, see if you can notice a little Eastern European influence Satchmo occasionally flavors this record with. Some writers believe this musical flavoring originated in his time with the Lithuanian Karnofskys. After all, sixty years later Louis wrote, "It was the Jewish family who instilled in me singing from the heart."

Another song in a minor key with a bit of Karnofsky flavoring is "Chim Chim Cheree." Pops almost always stuck to tunes in a major (happy) key, so his extended take on this Disney tune is fairly rare. Plus there's the unmistakable joy he has in singing "a-chimmie-chimmie-chimmie."

4   Now You Has Jazz

in which Louis shows us we can
go with the flow when the unexpected occurs

It doesn't get any more ciché than this: "When life hands you a lemon . . ." You know the rest. Never mind that some of us *like* lemons, it's often hard to see an unexpected change as an opportunity. But making lemonade is just what Satchmo did many times in his storied career.

For one example, let's travel back to 1926 Chicago, the heart of the Roaring Twenties. Louis had been a sensation there, gone and made his mark in New York, then returned to become an even bigger star in the capital of the Midwest. He put together a group of the best New Orleans musicians he could gather, to create a series of records now acclaimed as some of the greatest ever made. It was in making these records that Louis really started to soar and established jazz as a soloist's art. (Also, it's from these small group sessions that NASA chose the recording now zipping out of our solar system on the Voyager spacecraft.)

Picture Louis in an early recording studio with a

trombonist, clarinetist, pianist, and banjo player arranged around a big horn like that of a Victrola (the old, acoustic type of record player). Their sound waves would be funneled to a stylus cutting a long, spiral groove into a rotating wax master disc. After making a mold from this master, many copies of a record could be pressed. Louis and the group were recording a song called "Heebie Jeebies," a slang term for feeling anxious or excited. While playing the happy-sounding, medium tempo piece, the unexpected occurred. To stop the "take" and start the whole thing over would waste a master disc. Let's let Louis himself tell how he salvaged the situation:

> I dropped the paper with the lyrics – right in the middle of the tune . . . And I did not want to stop and spoil the record which was moving along so wonderfully . . . So when I dropped the paper, I immediately turned back into the horn and started to Scatting . . . Just as nothing had happened . . . When I finished the record I just knew the recording people would throw it out . . . And to my surprise they all came running out of the controlling booth and said – "Leave That In."

This is the creation myth of scat singing, an element of jazz in which, you might recall, a singer improvises with meaningless syllables in place of words. (Feel free to leave for a minute and listen to "Heebie Jeebies" on the companion website.) This wasn't the first scat singing on record as many believe, much less the first scat singing ever. But Louis's spirit and inventiveness sure put it on the map, selling an unheard-of 40,000 copies. In fact, it's called "scat" singing because that's a particular syllable Pops used on the record. When Louis starts scatting, there are no words getting in the way, for our conscious minds to interpret. We're about as directly in touch with another's joy as we can be, like hearing my kids yell, "Woo hoo!" when finding out they're going to the beach. But with Louis the joy is improvised artistically, with a banjo in the background. It doesn't get much better than that.

Hello, Hit Record

For a second example of adapting to the unexpected, we'll jump ahead forty years or so. But we'll bring that banjo with us, since it plays a role in another key recording in Louis's life. By late 1963 Louis's group, the All Stars, had toured all over the world and were in great demand around the country and on TV. Still, Louis and his manager craved another hit record that would get significant radio play, as had happened with "Blueberry Hill" in the late 1940s and "Mack the Knife" in the '50s. He hadn't recorded anything for a couple of years, and the producer decided to have him record a couple of contemporary show tunes. The first seemed tailor-made for the pop charts. "A Lot of Livin' to Do" was from the popular show and movie *Bye Bye Birdie*. It had a fun beat and lyrics about going out and living large. A no-brainer for Satchmo, in other words. The only other tune scheduled for the session was from an obscure (as in "hadn't-even-opened-yet") musical by a little-known composer, Jerry Herman. Louis and the boys would record the title song.

Pops didn't much care for it. It seemed too plain. He even changed a few lyrics, throwing in his own name. Nevertheless the record seemed bland. The call went out for a banjoist to add a little flavor. He soon arrived and added an intro, and the record was made. Pops promptly forgot about both tunes, and Kapp Records released the single with "Livin'" as the A-side. On the B-side was that song Louis thought too simple: "Hello, Dolly."

The Broadway show opened in early 1964 and became a huge hit in New York. That, plus the excellence of Louis's record, led to his getting some serious airplay on the radio. But the All Stars were out on tour in the Midwest, literally out of the loop. Pretty soon they were getting requests from their audiences for "Hello Dolly." It was such an obscure thing when they had recorded it, Louis couldn't even remember what it was. Arvell Shaw, his bassist, reminded him and they looked around for the lead sheets (sketched-out written parts) from the recording session. Lost. They telegrammed their office in New York: What to do? The answer: go buy a copy of their own recording so they could learn their own tune. But the record was selling like proverbial hotcakes; they looked and looked, but there was none to be found. The office had to fly Louis a recording. The band listened to it several times, relearned their parts and played it that night.

Finally the crowd got what it wanted. Louis got eight curtain calls.

Perhaps you remember Paul Harvey, whose radio broadcast always told a story with one important detail left out. When he revealed it, he would intone in his inimitable way, "And now you know the *rest* . . . of the story." This story likewise has one last little twist like that. The record of "Hello, Dolly" grew and grew in popularity until it became one of those records where you couldn't avoid it if you tried. It rose on the charts until it reached number one in May 1964, the last number one recording by a jazz artist (who was also the oldest person ever to reach that top spot). Biographer Terry Teachout believes it was the amazing success of this record that propelled Louis from jazz star to cultural icon. Since "Hello Dolly" became the number one record, that means Louis must have knocked a previous act out of first place. Who was that group he toppled from first place, which they had held for fourteen weeks? A relatively new act from overseas, a little group with funny haircuts and an oddly-spelled name: the Beatles.

Another, Cheesy Food Metaphor

In both stories, Louis adjusts to the unexpected. The first curveball is pretty small, a dropped piece of paper. But he hits a home run. Another artist might have said, "Hold it. Cut. Set up a new master and let's take it from the top." But Louis starts scatting. The second unexpected event is a bit more challenging: audiences demanding an unknown tune, and the musicians having to scurry to find and relearn it. But relearn it they do, bringing joy to thousands of hearers.

Aside from these two anecdotes, in his career Louis had to make other, more substantial adjustments to change. In the mid-1930s, a decade and a half of playing the trumpet hard every night caught up with Pops and he suffered lip injuries. Though he kept his high notes, he was never quite as nimble as in the twenties. So he and his record label had him focus more on pop songs and singing (though of course he kept on trumpeting, too). After World War II, tastes and economics changed. Big swing bands were no longer viable. Many were folding. Few big band leaders would retain their place in the public eye after the war. But Louis did. He changed with the times. Though he hated to lay off a dozen or more men, he formed a small group and became the highest-paid act in jazz.

But he didn't retreat back to early New Orleans-style music, even though his group looked like that type of combo. And though he didn't embrace the new, intellectual be-bop style of the late 1940s and '50s (he *had* been playing since 1913, after all) his style and repertoire did change with the times. Once when listening to an old recording of a good early jazz group, Louis and his musicians broke up in laughter at how dated and corny it sounded. Some people criticized his All Star concerts for being predictable. True, the group always opened the same way (not an unusual practice), and the hits Louis *had* to play did add up over the years. But perusing his programs over two decades of shows, critics find great variety, with the group continually dropping and adding songs, including many then-current pop tunes. Louis Armstrong the self-avowed Beatles fan even recorded John Lennon's "Give Peace a Chance" in 1970! Louis could have stagnated or gone backwards after the big band era collapsed. But his resilience resulted in his becoming even more popular as he aged, like a fine wine.

Or a fine cheese, our second food metaphor in this chapter on adjusting to change. One common phrase for new circumstances being imposed on you is "having your cheese moved." This metaphor entered pop culture in the late 1990s thanks to Spencer Johnson's bestselling book, *Who Moved My Cheese?* It's a little tale of two mice and two people who live in a maze and get used to where the cheese always is. One day it's gone. How will they handle it? Spoiler alert: the moral of this a-mazing tale is, "Change happens, go with the flow." But that's easier said than done, which is probably the reason for the book's millions of readers. Though we like variety in little things, we generally prefer consistency in how the world works. This probably harkens back to thousands of years of living in the wild, where the unexpected could be not only bad but possibly life-threatening.

Moreover, the unexpected is especially troubling when it is imposed from the outside. Notice the title is not, "Hey, my cheese moved." No, *someone* has moved it, forcing you to adjust, reminding you you're not in control. If you want to annoy someone fast, tell them they have to learn a new way to do something they've been doing for a while. Even young people. I got quite a chuckle when Facebook changed its format and I overheard my high school students complaining about it. "Why do they always have to change everything?!" Just wait, kids. Just wait.

Change and the unexpected often mean work: time and energy spent on something we'd rather not be doing, like learning a new system at the office, how to program a new phone, even how to place your garbage when the city gets new trucks. In my field, it's online teaching, a pretty big move of the cheese, a game changer, really. Even when our rational minds can see there will be a benefit to the change (as there certainly is to online learning), there's an annoyance that accompanies having to do things differently. In fact, perceiving the need to adjust to something is one of the key components of stress, especially when you're in doubt about your ability to meet the challenge successfully. Even positive changes we choose to make can be stressful. Try getting married or having a child.

But as Dr. Johnson points out in his fable, change is a fact of life. Shift happens. And the rate of change, the speed at which things are shifting is itself speeding up. Even *change* is changing! For several hundred thousand years as *Homo sapiens*, change was rarer and slower. You lived as your ancestors had, with pretty much the same beliefs, customs, and technology. Now, even a decade ago can seem almost like another world. Compare the Archie-n-Jughead malt shop culture of 1960 to post-Woodstock 1970. And for our long-ago ancestors, when change did happen, it was often predictable and orderly, like the procession of the seasons or migration of prey. Ironically, people could order their lives around change. Now in many areas, especially technology, the rate of change is exponential and unpredictable, at least to most laypeople. Living happily in 1994, I had no idea that in 2000 I'd be buying Christmas presents and getting my news via some newfangled "interweb" gizmo. So, unlike our ancestors who dealt with predictable, cyclic changes, we really don't know what accelerating alterations will bring. The cheese is being moved faster and faster, and it's mutating into new kinds we've never tasted before.

This is not what we're designed or evolved for. But it's how things are. We can curse the dark or light a candle; complain about the moving cheese, or lace up our sneakers and run with it. Louis was obviously a sneaker-lacer. Since faster, unexpected change is now the status quo and since it is by nature stressful, how can we be more like Louis and go with the flow?

How to Be More Resilient

The American Psychological Association has produced a helpful online resource with some good suggestions on how to be better at rolling with the flow. One is to accept that the unexpected is very much part of life. Permanency is an illusion and a craving (more on this in Practices at the end of this chapter). The sooner we acknowledge that change and the unexpected are everywhere, the better we can adapt. It's also helpful if you're stressing about the change to acknowledge and say to yourself, "I'm worrying and stressing about this change. It's a very natural reaction." You are by no means a bad or odd person for resisting change or disliking the unexpected, especially if it does come with very challenging consequences. But it will help if you consciously acknowledge the change and your response as being what they are.

You can also purposefully keep things in perspective. You can think of people who are facing worse. And you can consciously try to see the potential positives. This gets back to the "make lemonade" idea. In my profession's paradigm shift to online teaching, though it could result in jobs lost, there will be other positions created. And though I might miss the fun my students and I have in class, I might also welcome not having to be the behavior manager of thirty teenagers forced to be in the same room for an hour.

Aside from this cognitive (thought) work of accepting the unexpected and looking for positives, another suggestion is to take some concrete action. Even if you never come to *embrace* unexpected change (again, a quite natural response), you can still do something. When the cheese moves, your chance of starving goes up dramatically if you do nothing. Taking even a small step toward the new cheese will increase your chance of future success, plus you'll feel much better than worrying or doing nothing. I can worry about the trend towards online teaching or I can take a summer course on how to do it. Even though I'd rather be kayaking (or writing about Louis), just that small bit of progress will reduce my worrying and make me more likely to succeed as the changes happen. And rolling with one change will make me more resilient in future disruptions.

Look around your world: family, work, religion, public affairs, even sports. What are changes you can see coming either now or in the future? You can acknowledge that change is unavoidable and that these specific changes are happening. And you can do something, even something small to adjust to them. You have adjusted to change in the past and you can again in the future. Who knows? Maybe your new cheese will eventually make you burst into some joyful scat singing!

Practices

One way to cling less to the status quo is first to recognize the attachment; then consciously remember the impermanence of all things. Think of any aspect of your life and you can probably remember pretty quickly how it used to be different. And the permanence of you? Forget about it. You're constantly dying and being reborn at the cellular level. Even your nerve cells, which don't die and reproduce, still over time exchange the matter that makes them up. That exchange is what makes "life" life after all. So even once you reach adulthood, there will still be several more "yous," considering just the physical body and its matter. And that's totally aside from how we change mentally and emotionally over the years.

Even the most solid, nonliving physical object is really an event. Remember your chemistry. Any seemingly-solid stone you hold in your hand is mostly empty space down at the atomic level. And its tiny little atoms are all in motion. All is in motion. All is change.

Here is an easy guided relaxation practice, to help remember our true state of impermanence and to be more resilient.

Sit comfortably in a quiet room. Notice your breathing. Let your mind be as relaxed as you can.

Wait about three breaths. After that, use this pair of sentences from a renowned teacher of spirituality, Thich Nhat Hanh:

Each time you inhale, think,
"Breathing in, I calm my body."

As you exhale, think,
"Breathing out, I smile."

Don't force a smile, but don't try to stifle it if one arises. Take the eminent philosopher Paul McCartney's advice and let it be. Breathe at whatever tempo feels natural; your body will do what's right for you. You can even use shorthand after a few breaths, simply thinking "calm" on the in-breath, "smile" on the out.

After several repetitions of that pair of thoughts, try moving through the following sequence about impermanence. Do each set a few times until it seems right to move on. Trying to count a specific number of "reps" will only distract you. You can visualize what the words mean or not. When your thoughts wander, just return gently to the exercise.

Seeing my body being born, I breathe in;
Smiling to my body being born, I breathe out.

Seeing my cells living and dying, I breathe in;
Smiling to my cells living and dying, I breathe out.

Seeing my atoms in motion, I breathe in;
Smiling to my atoms in motion, I breath out.

Seeing myself as an event, I breathe in.
Smiling to myself as an event, I breathe out.

Seeing my body returning to dust, I breathe in.
Smiling to my body returning to dust, I breathe out.

Then arise, go forth, and live your life. You'll be calmer, mentally sharper, and a bit less attached to the way things are. The five pairs of thoughts above are my own, provided as a starting place for you. Nhat Hanh has written many sets of these meditations, about all different aspects of life including emotions and healing. You'll find them in his wonderful, practical little book, *The Blooming of a Lotus*.

Listening Suggestions

Links to audio and video files are found at
www.livelikelouis.com.

"Heebie Jeebies" is described pretty well in the chapter, as is "Hello Dolly."

It surprised me to learn Pops had recorded John Lennon's "Give Peace a Chance." In my perfect world, someone is about to unearth a trove of unknown tapes of Louis doing an album's worth of Beatles songs. Barring that, we'll have to settle for this one, written by one of the lads Louis displaced in 1964. It's an odd record, really. On second thought, maybe it's better if those imaginary tapes remain buried.

Changing with the times also involved recording the title song for the James Bond film *On Her Majesty's Secret Service.* We get to hear Satchmo in a typical-sounding, late-sixties pop arrangement. This is the first recording made after a long hospital stay, but Louis sounds fine here, neither shaken nor stirred.

5   Swing That Music

in which Louis and some high notes show us
we can be confident in our talents
and grow our gifts

Ever pay someone a compliment and have them
dismiss it? You say they did a good job, and they
respond that anyone might have done as well. Or
that it was "really nothing." Or that some part of it
could have been better. Louis Armstrong on the
other hand – though far from arrogant – was confident in his talent. He accepted his strengths, and
this was one of the ingredients of his success in
bringing joy to millions.

It was in late 1924 after the breakup of King
Oliver's band in Chicago that Satchmo went to the
Big Apple to be a featured player in the top black
dance band there. But after a few weeks, he knew
his talent wasn't being used to its full extent. He'd
been singing all his life, and his new leader, Fletcher
Henderson, really wasn't interested in what Louis
had to offer that way. The few times Louis sang, it
went over very well, but it never became part of the
band's routine. Plus, Henderson limited Louis's

cornet soloing to a few measures at a time. Though he was now in a premier band, Louis felt stifled. His wife, Lil, the college-educated piano player he had met in Oliver's band, was still in Chicago. She wrote to him that she had assembled a new group and wanted him to return and be its star. Louis hesitated. He maintained all his life that he hadn't wanted to be a star. But it meant better money. And his wife was, shall we say, a rather persuasive woman. She had been the driving force in Louis's leaving for New York in the first place. Now, with the opportunity for her husband to advance his (and her) fortunes even further by returning to Chicago, she sent him a pointed telegram: "Come by starting date or not at all."

Come he did.

And become a star, he did too. First in person, billed as "World's Greatest Cornet Player" on a huge sign (placed by his wife) he loathed. Then on record with his Hot Five discs selling out nationwide. In 1926 Louis was packing 'em in at the Dreamland club. Musicians were flocking to hear this phenom, enjoying his mastery and checking his horn to make sure his pyrotechnics weren't a trick. There was no trickery, just talent and hard work. Louis was nothing if not hardworking. For in addition to playing in nightclubs, he joined an orchestra that played in between the silent pictures at the Vendome Theater, the largest movie palace on Chicago's South Side. Here as on the riverboats, Louis played all kinds of music. But his special role was to be featured on the "hot" numbers. Leader Erskine Tate encouraged him to shine, even forcing him to go onstage lit by a spotlight. It was at the Vendome that Pops, always the entertainer, learned to use his trumpet's high range to thrill a crowd. He began his habit of repeating a high note 100 or more times. The audience would go wild, counting them all as he reeled them off. Then he'd slide up to an even higher note to end the piece and bring down the house. Later asked if he had been nervous about missing the note, Louis confidently replied, "I had it in my pocket all the time."

Negativity Comes Naturally

Not all are as confident in their abilities and accomplishments. Though American education and upbringing often teach children to assess their strengths and feel like winners (sometimes to extreme), many of us were taught that acknowledging our strengths was akin to bragging, and that we shouldn't think too much of ourselves. There is quite a contrast between the World War II generation, famous for humbly maintaining they were not heroes and only did what had to be done; and the mode now where every player gets a medal, and a B on a spelling test can be accompanied by a sticker proclaiming it "Awesome!" And yet there are still plenty of folks who would be hard pressed to acknowledge even a couple of strengths, or might feel it embarrassing or wrong to do so. But ask people where they're deficient or how they might improve, and stand back as the words start flowing. We're naturally attuned to negatives and deficiencies in general and we do not exclude ourselves. Psychiatrist David Burns calls our focusing on how we should be better a "shouldy" approach to life. (Say the word aloud to get the full effect of the pun.)

The former United Methodist bishop in Michigan, Rev. Donald Ott, once told a story of a young piano genius who walks offstage to wild applause after a concert. The custodian backstage remarks, "Listen to that, everyone's applauding." "No," the artist remarks glumly, "there's one who's not, way up in the balcony: my teacher." Bishop Ott remarked that very often we are that teacher, the one person disapproving of ourselves, even when others are appreciating what we've done or who we are. Even among our youth, where narcissism is measurably on the rise, there's still plenty of self-doubt to go around. I wish I had a free iTunes song credit for every time I've heard a high school Calculus student call herself dumb, or a student in Advanced Placement English declare himself bad at writing.

Psychologists tell us this is probably natural. Our ancient ancestors who noticed problems and dealt with them were more likely to survive and pass on their genes. If a band of cave-dwellers just sat around admiring their paintings and bearskin tunics, but failed to notice a hole in their defenses, they probably wouldn't survive too long. And so we inherit a survival strategy to notice deficiencies and not feel satisfied with good conditions. But life is beyond survival now. At least in the developed world with its social safety nets, physical survival is not really the issue. Now many of us have time and energy to use for personal growth and contributing to larger wholes, whether by taking piano lessons, reading to third-graders, or joining our local chapter of Ducks Unlimited. And when you're beyond true survival mode, the evidence is clear that it's far more effective to concentrate on, and develop, your strengths. Yet, we often continue to focus on our faults and (maybe) try to fix them. It's a hard instinct to fight. The great psychologist Carl Jung liked to remark, "You can throw nature out with a pitchfork, but she always comes back with a vengeance."

Strengths-Based Is Wiser

However, in spite of our instinct to attend to negatives, recognizing and developing strengths is a more efficient and productive avenue to success. Perhaps you've tried to eliminate a bad habit, or harder still, change a character trait you don't like. It *can* be done, but the time and energy required are monumentally greater than that needed to improve a strength. It's like trying to push a car stuck in the mud with the wheels pointing the wrong direction. Building on a strength, however, is like a cross-country skier giving herself a push in the direction she's already heading. *Far* less energy is required.

In addition to being more efficient, building on strengths is much more likely to be successful. New Year's resolutions are famous for lasting only a couple of weeks, though they *are* good for the gym membership industry. Isn't it natural to resist someone telling you what to do? So when trying to correct our faults, we become the nagging parent to ourselves. Of course, we'll then (non-consciously) resist our own bossy self and disobey: "I'll show 'me' who's boss: I *will* eat that donut!" Plus if you're looking to change a character trait, those become more difficult to change the longer you've spent being that way. This raises the likelihood of failure, giving yourself one more thing to feel bad about, creating a vicious circle. The "doom loop," Jim Collins, author of *Good to Great*, calls it. Building on strengths, however, leads to what Collins calls the "flywheel effect," a positive feedback loop. Using and growing a talent leads to success, which feels good and leads to wanting to grow your positives even more. Simply put, recognizing and building on strengths is far more efficient and far more productive than correcting faults.

I know how weird it can feel to let your faults be, trust me. Your biological and cultural programming will keep bringing shortcomings to mind, urging you to eliminate them, whether extra pounds, a messy desk, or being on the compulsive side. Your inner voice will whisper, "That's wrong; fix it." But research shows both in the personal sphere and in business if you were to choose exclusively either to build on strengths or correct faults, the one who attends to maximizing talents will end up further along. Collins even advocates, at least in business, finding the *one* thing you really do best and focusing your energy and effort on that single, distinctive service or ability.

Lest this seem too head-in-the sand, many advocates of strengths-based thinking will still tell you if there is a fault truly sinking you, it must be addressed. If there's some hole in the boat causing you to go under, yes, fix the hole rather than spiff up the boat's nice paint job. We're talking literally about a character trait or behavior that's harmful to yourself or others. But most perceived weaknesses are not dangerous, either literally or figuratively; usually they're just annoying obsessions about how we could improve, often in comparison to others. Imagine the owner of a cruise ship worrying that it's not as nimble as a jet-ski, so she focuses on making it more maneuverable while letting its wonderful cuisine go stale. Or imagine a jet-ski owner worried that his agile little craft isn't swank like a cruise ship, so he adds a champagne flute to the dashboard. How much enjoyment would be lost, having to trim speed so as not to spill the bubbly? These are silly examples perhaps, but true in their essence: it's smarter to spend your limited energy on knowing, accepting, and building on your strengths. That's why strengths-based management, therapy, and education are here to stay: not just fads, but ideas whose time has come, thanks to their efficiency and success.

Louis Armstrong was aware of his abilities. His records sold out, the clubs were packed, people screamed for him, early "hipsters" even adopted his unique slang heard on some of the records. He later (accurately) recollected that his bandleader in New York hadn't recognized a million dollar talent when he had one. But Louis never lorded it over anyone, later thanking that leader for the opportunities he did give him. Later, when he himself was a leader, Pops was known for being easy to work with and having a gracious spirit toward other musicians. On those Hot Five records where Louis started taking extended, fantastic solos, he let the other musicians solo too. Decades later the same would be true for the All Stars. When some critics noted the lesser abilities of some of the musicians who filled out his big bands in the 1930s and '40s, Louis remarked that if a player was trying, Pops could overlook the man's weaknesses to hear the good. He likened his philosophy to that of a churchgoer who enjoyed a good preacher, but could still look past a poor one to hear Jesus in the attempt. He wrote,

> I have played with quite a few musicians who weren't so good. But as long as they could hold their instruments correct, and display their willingness to play as best they could, I would look over their shoulder and see Joe Oliver and several other great masters from my home town.

1953: Louis continued to hit the high notes throughout his career, though more selectively.

Likewise, it's been my experience, working at entertainment venues and in education, to find that most who are truly excellent in their field do know it, but are not arrogant. Once, oddly enough, I met dancer/singer/actor/choreographer/director Gene Kelly alone in a university hallway. Our short encounter ended with *him* thanking *me* for appreciating his wonderful films. The tantrum-throwing diva gets all the press, but for each of them, there are many more who are aware that their talents are gifts on loan for the good of others. The best teachers I have known have always been generous in complimenting others and sharing their insights. Recognizing and focusing on your strengths clearly doesn't make you a self-centered jerk. One might even argue that to deny your strengths and focus on your weaknesses is itself a form of arrogance, devaluing the gifts you've been given. Didn't a famous Jewish rabbi even tell a parable about valuing and using your talents?

Your strengths are real. They are good. It's unwise, maybe even wrong, to ignore or dismiss them. Your strengths are the means by which you may most effectively cooperate with the ever-expanding spirit of growth and love. Your strengths are the means by which you can make ours a more wonderful world.

Practices

If you recognize yourself as someone who focuses on negatives, try this exercise. Make a list of some personal failings or weaknesses that bug you: unhelpful habits, good qualities you lack, or negative ones you possess.

Then – and this might feel odd – next to each fault write, "Let it be." As described above, it's counterintuitive not to want to eliminate a weakness. But accepting your weaknesses can allow you to focus more on your strengths. It can also make you more tolerant of your fellow human beings' shortcomings. Even if it feels wrong to admit a failing and abandon the need to fix it, write "Let it be" anyway.

Another exercise, involving movement: Hold your hands like a bowl and imagine your perceived faults in it. Then raise your arms and open the bowl, releasing the concerns upwards. Say this paraphrase of a well-known affirmation by author and teacher Wayne Dyer:

"I release the need to determine how I should be."

If you are religious, admit that if these perceived failings are to be "fixed" it is up to God to do so. Let go and let God, as the saying goes.

Notice that we are not so radical as to say your faults are good things or even okay (though you might come to see them that way). It is merely acknowledging that they are as they are, and it is far more efficient and beneficial to others to grow your strengths. Now try writing a few of these:

I give thanks for my talent/strength of . . .

I can grow it, by . . .

I can use it for good, by . . .

Listening Suggestions

Links to audio and video files are found at
www.livelikelouis.com.

It's time to encounter Louis's sheer trumpet virtuosity. Many critics and fans consider "West End Blues" from 1928 to be Louis's magnum opus. It even gets its own segment in Ken Burns' epic film, *Jazz*. Louis opens with an extended cadenza, a long, seemingly free-form solo. The trumpet traces its lineage back to war horns, and Louis in effect is sounding a bugle call to the world, "I am here. We are here." Toward the end of the piece, Pops holds a long note, then without taking a breath goes right into some groundbreaking musical creation and physical agility. Critic Gunther Schuller wrote, "The clarion call of 'West End Blues' served notice that jazz had the potential capacity to compete with the highest order of previously known musical expression." A true three-minute masterpiece, if ever there was one.

1927's "Potato Head Blues" is another piece with great, nimble, humorous playing. Behind Louis's solo the band provides a good example of "stop-time," the meaning of which will be self-evident when you listen.

To introduce "Swing That Music," the quintessential 1930s Satchmo showpiece, I must quote from biographer and archivist Ricky Riccardi's terrific blog, *The Wonderful World of Louis Armstrong* (www.dipperouth.blogspot.com):

> If you take blood pressure medication, take it before proceeding. If you have a bad back, now is a good time to strap yourself in tight to your chair. If you have bad breath, chew some gum, for heaven's sake. Okay, all ready, kids? Let's proceed with (drum roll please) "Swing That Music."

Here is Louis the Star Trumpeter strutting his stuff in 1936 on a song that would be thoroughly forgettable if not for Pops' marvelous trumpet work. Riccardi writes that it "displays his free-form sense of rhythm as it often floats above the frantic beat." During his last chorus you can hear Louis doing that thing he did to drive crowds wild, first in Chicago, then across the country and in Europe: a series of repeated high notes. In this case, for you musicians in the audience, it's forty-two concert high C's sliding up to a high E-flat for the finale.

Some critics think acclaim lured Louis away from the more creative solos of his 1920s recordings into a predictable rut of just belting out high notes. Notice, however, that he keeps them in his pocket for most of the record. Before them, his solo is really quite fluid, saving the repeated high C's for the ending. Louis was one star who knew what he was doing.

6   That's My Home

*in which Louis and his wife, Lucille,
remind us to appreciate our home*

In the late 1930s Louis got an extended gig playing
at the famous Cotton Club nightspot in Harlem.
One of the dancers, Lucille Wilson, caught his eye.
Louis found her very attractive, plus she seemed
very down-to-earth for someone in entertainment.
Here was a young woman with no real aspirations
to stardom, dancing only to support her mother and
siblings, even selling cookies to the entertainers
every evening. The smitten Louis started buying all
her cookies each night.

He decided to make a move. If you're ever in
need of a pick-up line, here's how Louis recalled
approaching Lucille. It doesn't get much more
straightforward than this: "Lucille, I might as well
tell you right now, I have eyes for you, and have
been having them for a long time. And if any of
these cats in the show [are] shooting at you, I want
to be in the running." It worked. The fact that Louis
was an extremely personable guy and a star entertainer probably didn't hurt either. After asking if

the Northern girl could cook red beans and rice, he invited himself over for dinner, ate "like a dog," and the courtship was on. They wed in 1942.

By that time, Louis had been away from his only home, New Orleans, for twenty years. He had lived in hotels and apartments. Lucille, however, didn't aspire to an entertainer's rambling existence, but to a stable middle-class life. Though she joined Louis on the road, living out of suitcases, it just wasn't to her tastes. At Christmastime she got an inkling that Louis himself would appreciate some stability. While Louis was on stage she set up a small tree in their hotel room. When he returned, Lucille recalled,

> he took one look at it and he just clammed up, you know? Louis isn't very emotional; he doesn't say much when he's over-whelmed. . . . We went to bed. And Louis was still laying up in bed watching the tree; his eyes just like a baby's eyes would watch something.

It was his first Christmas tree.

The next day, the band was due in another town, so Lucille was going to leave the tree. Louis, however, would have none of it. Lucille ended up carting the tree from hotel room to hotel room well into January. Louis even wanted it mailed home, and his wife had to convince him that was unworkable.

In 1943, after Lucille had returned to New York ahead of Louis, she went to the working-class Corona neighborhood of Queens. There she purchased a house from a white family she had known as a girl. It was a fairly imposing structure, two stories with a squared-off roofline, suggesting to my Midwestern eyes a segment of a townhouse. Architecture aside, there's a small twist in the tale: Lucille bought it without Louis's knowledge, giving him only an address to seek when done touring.

After many days on the road, Louis's band bus arrived in New York. He hired a cab and gave the cabbie the address. One long ride later, Louis arrived in the sedate, racially-mixed Queens neighborhood, a far cry from Harlem. He thought the cabbie either had gotten it wrong or was fooling him, but he was tired and in no mood for jokes. "One look at that big, *fine* house, and right away I said to the driver, 'Aw, man, quit kidding and take me to the address that I'm looking for.'" But he took a chance and went up to ring the doorbell. Who should open the door but Lucille in a silk nightie and curlers?

She showed him around the home she had bought and decorated. Louis loved the house, especially appreciating the care Lucille had put into furnishing it. "The more Lucille showed me around the house the more thrilled I got. . . . Right then I felt very grand all over it all. A little higher on the horse (as we express it). I've always appreciated the ordinary good things." After twenty years on the road, Louis had a real home.

He didn't spend too many days there at any one stretch until the last few years of his life. It was more Lucille's house than his, but Pops knew he had a home, a stable life awaiting him whenever he came off the road. In his later years, he loved being in his upstairs den listening to records and writing many long letters and personal essays there. On his state of the art tape recorders, he made 650 reel to reel tapes of readings, music, impromptu monologues, and discussions with friends. Then he would decorate the tape boxes in a fascinating collage style using photos, clippings, and other bits and pieces. In the 1950s Louis even collaged-over the walls in his den. Unfortunately, the ever-tasteful Lucille had them removed.

You can actually visit Louis's inner sanctum and soak up some Satchmo karma. His beloved house is not only still there, it's a wonderful museum, operated by Queens College. It's restored to look just as it did when Louis and Lucille lived there, including a turquoise "kitchen of the future" and a gold-fixtured bathroom featured on the show "Lifestyles of the Rich and Famous."

But no matter how fine and decorated it might be, a house is not a home. That takes people and the life they live together. Though Louis had three wives before Lucille, the fourth time was the charm. Louis and Lucille stayed together 'til Louis's death parted them in 1971. Louis wrote in a private letter,

> I love my wife, Lucille + she loves me. Or else we wouldn't have been together this long. Especially doing the crazy things I usually do for kicks. That's why I love her, because she's smart. The average woman would have quit my ol' ass – long, long ago.

Lucille was in her twenties when they were wed, but the Armstrongs never had children of their own. This was not through any lack of trying, if we believe Louis's many candid remarks about their love life. Louis did have an adopted son, though. When he was fourteen Louis had taken it upon himself to support his sick cousin, Flora, who had been taken advantage of by an older white man. Louis and his relatives were unable to afford the doctor's two-dollar fee. Flora died, but not before entrusting her baby to Louis's care by naming the child Clarence Armstrong.

Louis took his duties very seriously. At age seventeen when he married for the first time, he adopted Clarence, too. Clarence was mentally handicapped, which Louis blamed on a fall off a high, wet porch when he was three. Nevertheless, when he moved to Chicago Louis sent for Clarence and raised him, keeping Clarence with him as he went through two more marriages. Eventually Clarence was installed in a home of his own in the Bronx, which Louis visited often.

Home Includes the Neighborhood

Louis spent most of his life on the road until his last years. But he and Lucille were still an integral part of their Queens neighborhood for decades. Louis wrote in 1970 how Lucille would roast a turkey or ham for neighbors when there was a death, and how he enjoyed walking two blocks to Joe's Artistic Barber Shop for a trim. Dinner at his favorite Chinese restaurant would often grow cold due to the number of autographs he'd sign for neighbor kids. Those children were very important. He wrote,

> During my 54 years traveling on the road playing one night stands, and when I would return home, all of those kids in my block would be standing there right in front of my door waiting to help me unload my luggage and take it into the house.

Close friend Phoebe Jacobs recounts how when Louis came home off the road, "very often the neighbors would have banners out, 'Welcome Home, Pops.'" On nice days "he'd sit on the front steps of his house and buy kids Good Humors. And he'd ask them, 'Was your homework good? Were you a good boy?'"

Pops had a little balcony off his den and would play his horn there in the evening. If a couple of days went by without hearing his trumpet, neighbors would call and ask about his health. Lucille would let them know he was merely occupied with other matters. Once when his health truly wasn't good, after being released from the hospital with heart problems, neighborhood adults and children alike were careful to be quiet in the vicinity of the Armstrong residence. Their respect made quite an impression on Louis.

In the 1950s and '60s, Louis went from being a star to being an American institution. Lucille and his manager tried to get him to move, either to a bigger house in a neighborhood outside the city, or out to sunny Los Angeles, capital of the entertainment biz. Louis was adamant: he would not be moved. The home in Queens was fine enough for him, and he wasn't one to put on airs:

> We don't need to move out in the suburbs to some big mansion. . . . What for? What the hell I care about living in a "fashionable" neighborhood? Ain't nobody cuttin' off the lights and gas here 'cause we didn't pay our bills. The Frigidaire is full of food. What more do we need?

Plus, he treasured the specific connections he had made with the people in his neighborhood. Why cut those ties just for a "nicer" address and swimming pool? Pops remarked,

> We've both seen three generations grow up in our block where we bought our home in Corona, white and black, and those kids when they grew up and got married – their children – still come around to our house and visit their Uncle Louis and Aunt Lucille.

The regard people in his "Elmcor" neighborhood had for Louis is seen in a very touching photograph taken just after his death. A group of Little Leaguers holds homemade signs reading "Elmcor loves you," "Elmcor will never forget our Louie," and "Satchmo will live forever in our community."

Wanting What You Have

True confession time: these stories about Lucille, Louis, their home, and how he treasured it are the tales from this book I most need to hear. Not that I don't need the reminders we find in the other chapters. But valuing my home and family comes hard to me. In fact as I write this, it's summer vacation for us teacher-types, and where am I? At school, writing. Why? It's quiet. You see, I'm an introvert who likes calm and order. At my relatively small house are three teenagers, their friends, their stuff, two cats, and a dog: not exactly the recipe for calm and order. More like *The Family Circus*.

When the noise and clutter get to me, I find myself obsessing about what's wrong, rather than seeing and hearing what's right. I get to feeling like Jimmy Stewart's character, George Bailey, in the classic film *It's a Wonderful Life*, when he comes home in a dark mood. One kid is practicing the same song over and over on the piano, another is asking him how to spell some word, one is upstairs with a cold, and the little one keeps following him around saying, "'Scuze me." All that (plus his *really* bad day at work) makes him flip out. I know you've seen it: he yells at the kids and smashes a model of a bridge that's symbolic of his unrealized dreams of doing big things. Luckily George gets enlightened (by an angel named Clarence, ironically) and comes to see everything in a new light. Instead of bridges and fame, he enjoys a loving wife, decent kids, a roof over his head, and a town full of friends. He ends up wanting what he already has, which is a pretty sure recipe for real and lasting happiness.

Nicolas Cage portrays a man in a similar situation in *Family Man*. His character is a well-off single guy who wakes up in an alternate future, with kids bouncing on his bed in suburban Jersey. Though he initially wants his old single life back, he comes to appreciate the love that comes with the chaos. Some days I feel like *I* could use a visit from an angel to see what I'd be missing if life had turned out differently. I'll settle instead for the extended stay I'm getting with Satchmo and try to remember to use the practices at the end of this chapter.

I'm mindful that you who are reading this may be in a different situation, but still not treasuring your home. Perhaps your household feels not too noisy, but too empty. Or your apartment is too small, or your town is not to your liking. I would urge you, as I urge myself, to look on the positives that *are* there if we'll only have eyes and ears for them. Peace and quiet can give you important room to think or create or volunteer. Louis and Lucille were childless, but took it as an opportunity to bless many children in their neighborhood. A difficult neighbor or neighborhood can be an opportunity for prayer or service.

Very often no situation is absolute, but what we make of it. As Hamlet observes, there is nothing either good or bad but thinking makes it so. The Hebrew scriptures even tell us that as we think, so we are. The apostle Paul instructed a group of early Greek Christians that their life would be enhanced if they would see and focus on the good: "Whatsoever things are true, whatsoever things are honest, whatsoever things are just, whatsoever things are pure, whatsoever things are lovely, whatsoever things are of good report; if there be any virtue, and if there be any praise, think on these things." May you and I look for and think on whatever is good about our homes. Just like Louis.

Practices

Our attention is essentially a one-track system. While we are consciously focusing on the positive, we cannot – at that moment, anyway – be thinking of the negative. And since our thoughts and feelings interconnect, while we focus our thoughts on the positive we'll also feel better.

Take a few moments and jot down five things that could be viewed as good about your home or living situation. Write things about your household, family, dwelling, neighborhood, whatever. Bad things that aren't present also count (for example, "Our roof doesn't leak anymore").

If you get stuck for positives, acknowledge a negative feeling you presently have – no harm in being honest – then write a way it could be worse: "My house may be cramped . . . but at least the roof doesn't leak anymore." Or, "The dog is annoying to me . . . but she doesn't chew on my stuff."

If appreciating what you have is as difficult for you as it often is for me, remembering and writing your blessings will help you want what you already have. Try doing it several days in a row. You can expand it to other areas of negativity (if you have them) and make it a part of your morning routine. The repetition can even retrain your mind. What brain researcher Dr. Daniel Amen calls ANTs (automatic negative thoughts) can eventually be exterminated, replaced by positive thoughts.

Extra Credit

1. Buy an old 78 record of Louis's "That's My Home" via Ebay.

2. Hang it in a prominent place near your front door so you see it as you enter.

3. See how it affects you.

Yes, your author actually did this, and frankly, on its own, seeing the record every day didn't affect me much. But it looks cool and has started a number of conversations with guests wondering why I have an old Satchmo record hanging on the wall. Discussing Louis Armstrong can't help but raise a home's happiness quotient, right?

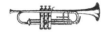

Listening Suggestions

Links to audio and video files are found at
www.livelikelouis.com.

I've seen "That's My Home" described as "saccharine" and I suppose it is. But Louis's 1932 recording of it is very moving, an example of his ability to transcend and transform the material he often had to work with. His friend and long-time bassist, Arvell Shaw, heard Louis's real self coming through every time Satchmo performed this number, one of his most requested tunes: "I listened not so much to the timbre of the voice, but to the *feeling*, because it was something that went deep inside. . . . When he would sing, 'I'm always welcomed back, no matter where I roam; it's just a little shack, to me it's home sweet home,' so help me I'd have to fight back the tears. Now *every night* we'd do that!"

Louis and Clarence

A friend advised me not to use specific website sources for these listening examples. But if there's any justice in the universe, Ricky Riccardi's aforementioned blog (dippermouth.blogspot.com) will be with us a long, long time. If anything ever qualified as a treasure trove, it's Ricky's blog: in-depth articles on Satchmo's recordings and life, with countless rare recordings and video clips. If you access it and search for the June 15, 2008 (Father's Day) entry, you'll be rewarded with an audio clip from a very early TV show featuring Louis and his son, Clarence. Ricky is right, in his observation that Louis's pride and love for Clarence come shining through, even in a one-minute exchange.

7   It's a Most Unusual Day

*in which Louis and a certain product
remind us to be ourselves
and not worry too much what others think*

We've gone six chapters without acknowledging a serious fact about Louis Armstrong. It's time to face the music: Louis was an addict. Yes, an addict . . . to an herbal remedy named Swiss Kriss: in short – a laxative. A *very* strong laxative. Louis's relationship to his beloved Swiss Kriss, and his evangelistic zeal in promoting it, can help us remember to relax and care a bit less what other people think of us.

Louis had been raised as many people were in his day to take a regular dose of "physic" in order to stay a "regular fellow." His mother, Mayann, trained him and his sister to do this at an early age. Louis recalled Mayann instructing them that because of "the food that you all eat today, you must take a good purge and clean your little stomachs out thoroughly. They will keep the germs away." Louis and his sistrer "both gave Mayann our word that we would stay physic-minded for the rest of our lives."

And so he did. In 1918 Louis did not succumb to the Spanish flu pandemic, but helped take care of the people in his neighborhood who were ill. He attributed his immunity to being "physic-minded" and taking that weekly dose of laxative. Given the lack of sanitation and refrigeration back then, who knows? Maybe he was right.

Louis writes about laxatives in his autobiography five times, which might seem odd. (It seemed so to me, frankly.) In fact, it might seem odd for someone to write about laxatives even once. Another perspective, however, is to remember what a normal part of life going to the bathroom is, and acknowledge that Louis had no problem writing about this natural function. In his many preserved letters and interviews, he discusses everything, all aspects of life: food, music, sex, sleep, health, and yes, bowel movements. I get the feeling that he was very natural in the sense that life was whole and integrated for him – it was not segmented and partitioned, with some topics off-limits.

He certainly had no trouble promoting Swiss Kriss. It's an herbal concoction still available even in my small city's only health food store. He discovered it in the writings of a health guru in the 1950s. The ingredients reminded him of the herbs his mother picked in New Orleans to clean out her children's systems. So he switched to it from his long-time purgative, Pluto Water (a lovely concoction whose ads featured the devil and the slogan, "When nature won't, Pluto will!"). Like many converts, he became something of a fanatic and gave out little packets of the highly effective Swiss Kriss to everyone he met, from friends to fellow musicians to audience members to diplomats, even to his nurses when he was hospitalized near the end of his life. He was especially happy he convinced the head nurse to try it, referring to her as "one of my toughest customers."

He often talked and wrote about Swiss Kriss, once proclaiming, "I take my Swiss Kriss, man, they keep you rollin'. Old Methuselah, he'd have been here with us if he had known about them." In a printed flyer to promote his diet methods, he gave instructions for getting started on Swiss Kriss.

> Your first dose will be real heavy to start blasting right away, and get the ball to rolling. . . . Don't get frantic because you have to trot to the bathroom several times when you first get up (awakened). P.S. You won't need an alarm clock to awaken you, no-o-o-o. . . . When you and Swiss Kriss get well acquainted, then you'll dig he's your friend.

He later jokes that if Swiss Kriss sponsors a radio show for him, his opening will be, "This is Satchmo speaking for Swiss Kriss. Are you loosening?"

Louis even had himself photographed on the toilet with the picture cropped to appear as if we're seeing him through a keyhole. (His bare behind is just barely hidden.) Beneath the photo he attached a prominent "Satchmo-slogan" urging folks to "leave it all behind ya," and had hundreds of promotional copies printed up. Another of his favorite slogans (appropriate for a horn player) was "Keep blasting!" and he often signed his letters "Swiss Krissly yours." (Ironically, his other common signature referred to his favorite food: "Red beans and ricely yours.") One story has a musician in a taxicab trying to smoke Swiss Kriss, since Pops had told him the herbs were such good stuff!

Tony Bennett enjoys telling the story of being at a dinner with Louis Armstrong and members of the British royal family including Princess Alexandra and the Duke of Kent. Amid discussion after a sumptuous meal, the princess turns to Tony and asks, "Did you ever try this?" She's holding a packet of Swiss Kriss. Louis had distributed "this very ferocious laxative" to the royal family! As Bennett tells it, the royals start reading the instructions, realize what it is, and the entire dinner party cracks up with people falling on the floor from laughter. He describes the mayhem as "the funniest thing I've actually seen, funnier than any Laurel and Hardy scene."

Please note that Louis didn't go around recommending a laxative just to shock people. Being rude to people was not his style. He sincerely thought Swiss Kriss was good for you. He wanted you to know about it, so he'd tell you. He didn't care if some people might think it crude. With Louis, what you saw was what you got. For example, when he returned as a star to New Orleans in 1931, a white announcer refused to introduce a "colored" band on the radio. Louis grabbed the mike and did it himself. Playing for King George in England, he ignored protocol and acknowledged the royal presence, lightheartedly announcing a brief solo, "This one's for you, Rex." After shows, in his dressing room he would receive everyone from the local mayor to old friends from New Orleans wanting a handout, with Louis dressed in his underwear with a kerchief on his head. He addressed President Eisenhower as "Daddy" and was the same around the Pope as he was around his friends. In fact, a story circulated after Louis met the Pope in the 1960s: the pontiff asks if Louis and his wife have children. Louis replies, "No, Dad, but we're still wailin'."

Satchmo was thoroughly comfortable with who he was, the same person no matter his surroundings. He could easily have echoed the catchphrase of another great star of the thirties, a certain spinach-eating sailor man who often stated, "I yam what I yam."

Pops in his kerchief, backstage at the Aquarium, New York, 1946.

You can do less, well.

There's a lesson here for me because I have too often worried what other people think. I do realize it's natural to care what others think about us. We're social animals, so we're hard-wired to care about the esteem of others. Primitive people who had more support were more likely to survive and pass on their genes. And in no way am I saying that we should be inconsiderate of others' feelings. But worry a *bit* less about what other people might think of us? Good call.

One way caring too much about others' opinions can show itself is by taking on tasks you feel you "should" do, shouldering duties you imagine a "good person" would undertake, even if they're really not right for you. It might be serving on a committee, joining a community group, even doing things for your family. Service is very good, but can be over-done for the wrong reason, because you feel you "ought." This overextension often comes from caring about what others think, trying to fit some image of the "good" mother or son or employee or citizen. It seems especially tough for women to resist this; thanks to the hormone oxytocin, you female folk are generally more prone to be nurturing and attuned to others' needs. Plus, our culture tells each woman she should be a sexy wife, the world's best mom, and a success in her career, all at the same time!

I hope by this point in the book you can trust that I would never say we shouldn't do things for others; nor should we avoid clear matters of duty or necessity. Contributing to the well-being of others is the essence of a meaningful life. But taking on *too* much, for the wrong reasons, then burning out or being resentful does little good and possibly much harm. If you're like me, you know this, but still need to be reminded it's okay to say no to things. Rarely will people think less of you. And if they do, adopt a bit of the Satchmo attitude: Let 'em!

Recently I resigned from a faculty committee. I explained to my principal that I supported the group's focus, but it wasn't one I was passionate about. I told him that to be most productive I need to spend my energy in areas I'm truly enthused about. Not only did he understand (high school principals definitely understand about being pulled in too many directions), he commended my decision. I was putting into practice a phrase I learned several years ago, but which has really stuck with me: "Do less, well." It makes for a saner, more centered life, one not so much in the "spin cycle." The philosopher Thoreau advised us,

> Our life is frittered away by detail. Simplify, simplify, simplify! I say, let your affairs be as two or three, and not a hundred or a thousand; instead of a million count half a dozen, and keep your accounts on your thumb-nail.

When you simplify, you're more able to be one with life and serve others from the center – instead of just adding one more spinning plate or juggling ball to an already confusing mix.

But can you wear purple?

Caring too much about others' opinions can also result in avoiding doing things they might think odd. Again, this is very normal, but also stifling. I'm reminded of the poem "Warning," by Jenny Joseph. It inspired the Red Hat Society, that international organization of daring grannies. The speaker in the poem begins by warning hearers that when she is old she will wear purple. But why wait until then? I suppose if you're in the corporate world, it could hold back your career if you wore a purple suit. But certainly in your off hours you could go for it. Let "purple" stand for whatever people might think is a bit goofy or daft (for instance, say, talking about a laxative all the time or wearing a kerchief on your head in your dressing room).

That spirit of cutting loose and not caring so much about others' opinions is probably why the BBC found Ms. Jones' poem to be the United Kingdom's most popular post-war poem in a 1996 poll. Learning that the poem is of British origin really didn't surprise me, since the English are known for allowing themselves to be a bit eccentric, indulging in somewhat odd hobbies and tastes. We driven Americans could probably learn something. Even Star Trek fans.

You see, I am one of those, a Trekkie dating back to my babyhood in the late '60s. No, I can't recite Shakespeare or the Bible in the Klingon language as some fans can; but I have gone to a couple of conventions and dressed in a Star Trek uniform for the movie premiere in 2009. After the movie was out for a while, a discussion thread was started in an online Trek forum, asking if we fans were now wearing Star Trek shirts in public. Not costumes, mind you, just t-shirts. Many respondents replied that they still were not, concerned what people would think or say. Of all the people in the world, you'd think *Trekkies* wouldn't care what people think, right? But the urge not to stand out runs deep.

After reading that thread I promptly went and found one of my Trek shirts, and a great one at that: four pictures of Mr. Spock arranged a la Andy Warhol. I threw it on and, since it was summer, took my ten-year-old son to the beach. We parked near the skateboard area full of "cool" nonconformist kids all wearing similar black clothing in the hot sun. Right away, deep from the primitive regions of my brain, came bubbling up a feeling of being . . . conspicuous. I was a middle-aged man instantly transported back to 1979 in junior high wearing an uncool shirt. As I walked my son toward the beach, two arriving skateboarders passed us. One quietly said, "Nice shirt." She probably meant it, since the movie was popular and still fresh in people's minds. But I was far from sure at the time.

Not only did I feel conspicuous, I felt guilty about it, for I had set out deliberately to be myself and not care what others thought. Emotions are complicated. I should add that walking past beautiful and/or buff sunbathers didn't help me feel any cooler sporting my Spock shirt. It was a good experience, though – it reminded me how strong is the urge not to stick out, a power that can stifle you from being yourself. I do, after all, like Star Trek; I've never really been a "cool" guy anyway and I need to remember that's okay – and just enjoy being what I "yam."

I think I can safely assume that you, O reader, are not a Swiss Kriss devotee. And it's unlikely you're a fellow Trekkie. But I'll bet there *is* some quirk about you, a weird hobby or a certain style you might like to wear that's not exactly, shall we say . . . up to date. Maybe you just have a penchant for singing loudly while you do housework or eat a snack your family finds bizarre. You can follow Louis's example, disregard what people think, and be who you are.

Our world will be a bit more wonderfully purple for it.

Practices

Swiss Kriss Directions for Musicians

Found on the Liberty Hall Jazz Quartet's website, these directions seem to come authentically from Satchmo's fertile mind. For the life of me, however, I cannot track down the original source. Use at your own risk therefore; I am not a doctor, nor do I play one on TV!

    1. All Musicians: One tablet (1 tspn. fiber) before dawn;
    2. Big Band Leaders: An extra dose 1 hour before performance;
    3. Featured Vocalists: An extra dose 15 minutes before performance.

You can eliminate a stressor.

It's all right, even *good*, to do less. If you are in too many optional activities, you can give yourself permission to seek a calmer, more efficient life. Then explain it to whoever is in charge in those terms, that you simply need fewer doings in order to be better at what you stay doing. Most people are understanding (sometimes even a little envious) of someone with the courage to check out of the spin cycle.

You can wear purple.

Whatever is your purple, let me urge you to identify and "wear" it today. Even if it's a Spock shirt to the beach. Enjoy.

Listening Suggestions

Links to audio and video files are found at
www.livelikelouis.com.

"Mahogany Hall Stomp" is a very nice tune with a melody and solo once commonly memorized by jazz trumpet players. Mahogany Hall was a legendary brothel in New Orleans, which brings up one last thing about Louis's personality he didn't hide. He liked prostitutes. Not as a customer, just as a fellow human being. He had delivered coal to them as a boy, lived in a red-light district, even made a prostitute his first wife. So when on tour, especially in the South, he welcomed them into his dressing room along with everybody else, the local dignitaries, the hustlers, the ministers, everyone, and he made it clear they were welcome. He often gave them help. If anyone had a problem with that, so be it. Louis loved people, and prostitutes were people too.

8   *Black and Blue*

*in which Louis and a president show us
we can be courageous*

In our first chapter, we accompany the five-year-old Louis Armstrong as he first meets Jim Crow on a segregated streetcar in 1906. Segregation continued, of course, and now we jump forward about fifty years to an incident in which Louis willingly jeopardizes his career to fight ongoing discrimination. Through his bravery this man shows us that we too can act with courage when it comes time to take a stand.

The Race Situation in 1957

This is not the place for an in-depth retelling of the history of Jim Crow laws. They're familiar to most Americans, either through history class or life experience. We know of the separate (and substandard) drinking fountains, beaches, hospitals, and schools. Most harmful was the fact that those who were kept down were barred from voting due to literacy tests and poll taxes. They could not begin to change the rules that held them back. In the 1940s blacks went off to Europe to defeat Hitler's brand of racial superiority only to return and find America's version still going strong. In some ways, by the early fifties not much had changed since little Louis's streetcar ride.

We've seen how Satchmo was open to white musicians and how he dared to form and maintain an integrated band starting in 1947. But by no means was his head in the sand regarding the difficult state of race relations in his country. Writing near the end of his life, he recollected how sometimes in his childhood days, whites would get drunk and go hunting for a black man to shoot – *any* black man.

> They wouldn't give up until they found one. From then on, Lord have mercy on the poor darkie. Then they would torture the poor darkie, as innocent as he may be. They would get their usual ignorant Chess Cat laughs before they would shoot him down – like a dog. My, my, my, those were the days.

No matter his fame or status, no black man was immune to discrimination. Even in the North, Louis played in plenty of whites-only nightclubs. On tour in the South, segregated lodgings were the rule. During his triumphant return to New Orleans in 1931 he tried to host a dance at an army base for his black hometown fans, but was prevented at the last minute due to race. By the late 1950s, Pops had met the Pope, toured Europe and Japan, dined with royalty, and played for a crowd of 100,000 in Ghana. But he couldn't play in New Orleans. A new Jim Crow law there prohibited performances by integrated bands. In an interview, he described his feelings towards his hometown:

> I ain't goin' back to New Orleans and let them white folks in my own hometown be whipping on me and killing me for my hustle. . . . Ain't it stupid? Jazz was born in New Orleans. . . . And I can remember when it wasn't no crime for cats of any color to get together and blow. They treat me better all over the world than they do in my own hometown.

"I don't care if I never see New Orleans again," he declared. He kept his word, staying away until 1965 after passage of the federal Civil Rights Act. New Orleans is evidence now of how far we've come since then. If you're fortunate enough to take a plane flight to New Orleans, first off, your seat *won't* be assigned to you based on the color of your skin. Second, the airport where you'll land is named for a black man: the Louis Armstrong New Orleans International Airport! But in 1957 such progress was only just beginning.

As you probably know, in that year one of the most important skirmishes in the long fight for progress occurred in Little Rock, Arkansas. You might not know the school board had in fact voted to integrate the schools. But Gov. Orville Faubus couldn't bear to see that happen. He deployed the Arkansas National Guard to block the path of nine black students trying to attend Central High School. He was clearly violating the Supreme Court's *Brown v. Board* decision and the authority of the federal government. President Eisenhower expressed his displeasure. Nevertheless, the national guard troops stood for days in front of the school, barring the door to education and equal protection of the laws. Some residents joined them to scream and spit at the teens. Others held prayer services for peace. The whole country was watching, including citizen Louis Armstrong. After a lifetime of discrimination, enough was enough.

Why the Risk Was Great

Before we examine the action Louis took, we need to understand that it was indeed a risk. Accustomed as we are to celebrities sounding off on social issues today, this was not the norm then. Sports stars and entertainers stuck to their trade and generally kept their mouths shut. Partly this was just the times, and partly it was sage business practice not to alienate a segment of one's audience. By 1957 Louis's audience was mainly white.

In the 1920s his records had been devoured by blacks. His in-your-face, bravura style of playing had made him a hero for many, a fellow black who was making it in the whites' world. "There was something in that voice they appreciated, the pride of race," observed blues composer W.C. Handy.

People throughout Chicago's South Side and Harlem even started talking like him, learning his special lingo from the vocals and spoken-word portions of his many hit records.

But times change, and to younger black Americans of the postwar era, Louis seemed like a relic of a past they were trying to forget. Their tastes were moving on to early rhythm and blues on the pop side, and frenetic, intellectual "be-bop" on the jazz side. White tastes were moving his way, however. By the 1950s Louis's accessible, happy music had made him white peoples' favorite "Negro." A huge crossover star, he had been appearing in movies for years and had begun doing the myriad television appearances that would make him universally known. So, to speak up about racial injustice could cost him plenty in those very tense times, a period we often incorrectly remember as bland "happy days." In the paranoid aftermath of McCarthyism, at the height of the Cold War and in the midst of civil rights protests and backlash, it was quite a risky move for Louis to speak up. But seeing soldiers denying black children a fair education was the last straw.

What He Said

Louis was on tour in North Dakota in 1957, ironically the first black ever to stay in the Dakota hotel in Grand Forks. A young reporter disguised as a waiter snuck into his room. Louis warmed to the young man's gutsiness and opened up. It was not an unplanned outburst to be retracted later. Louis even signed off on the reporter's transcript of their conversation. He would not use the excuse – as public figures so often do now – that his words were taken out of context. His deliberate remarks were distributed by the Associated Press and printed in papers across the country:

> Mr. Armstrong said President Eisenhower had "no guts" and described Gov. Orval E. Faubus of Arkansas as an "uneducated plow boy." He said the President was "two-faced" and had allowed Governor Faubus to run the Federal Government. "It's getting almost so bad a colored man hasn't got any country," the Negro entertainer said.

We now know these strong words were even stronger in the original and cleaned up for the papers. The reporter, Larry Lubnow, has discussed their conversation in that hotel room, and suffice it to say that Louis called Gov. Faubus something considerably worse than a "plow boy." When asked about a planned tour of Russia for the U.S. State Department, Louis replied, "The way they are treating my people in the South, the Government can go to hell."

Reaction, as they say, was mixed. Jackie Robinson came forward to echo Pops' criticism of Eisenhower, while Sammy Davis, Jr., chided Louis for not speaking out earlier. Columnist Jim Bishop called Louis an "ingrate," and the University of Alabama cancelled a planned concert. President

Eisenhower didn't respond to Armstrong. He did respond to Faubus, however, with the presence of the 101st Army Airborne division to escort the Little Rock Nine to class. Louis, in turn, responded with some "class" of his own in a personal telegram to the president:

> Mr. President. Daddy if and when you decide to take those little negro children personally into Central High School along with your marvelous troops, please take me along[.] "O God it would be such a great pleasure I assure you." . . . You have a good heart. . . . Am Swiss Krissly yours Louis Satchmo Armstrong.

It turns out Louis's career did not suffer too adversely, though it certainly might have. Such had happened to Paul Robeson, the great black actor and singer who had criticized the United States and compared it unfavorably to the Soviet Union. Blacklisting was a fact of life in the 1950s, a major fear of entertainers. Nevertheless, as Louis put it several days after his initial comment, "When I see on television and read about a crowd spitting on and cursing at a little colored girl . . . I think I have a right to get sore and say something about it."

Opportunities for Courage, Here in Zombie Land

Fast forward from 1957 to now. Where are the opportunities for courage? In an interesting essay for

the *New York Times*, Chuck Klosterman perceived
that so many books and movies are featuring zombies lately because they stand for what we fear
about ourselves: that we are wage-enslaved, cubi-
cle-imprisoned drones. We appear fully human, but
are really just . . . zombies. Compared to our ancestors who lived lives fraught with real danger,
whether from beasts or invaders, most of us do lead
fairly safe lives. Not to say we don't have hardships
and discouragements, but our lives just don't seem
to call for real courage as much as our ancestors'
did. Maybe this is a misperception on our part.
Generations often feel they've gone soft compared
to their rugged forebears. Even Teddy Roosevelt's
generation in the 1890s felt that way, comparing
itself unfavorably to the "manly" Civil War generation that preceded it.

So maybe it's a case of rose-colored glasses in
reverse, but it sure seems true: leaving my "hut"
every morning to go motivate eleventh-graders to
learn about civics is simply not as dangerous as going off to hunt a wildebeest or defend the village
from the enemies across the bay. An essential element of humanity is courage. Where can you be
courageous these days?

In our lives there are still things that need doing, in both the personal domain and the larger, social sphere. Usually the cost is time and effort,
which equate to "work" or "perseverance," certainly good things. But sometimes the doing also
involves risk. *Now* you're talking "courage." Louis
Armstrong thought soldiers preventing kids from
being treated like human beings had to stop. What

he could offer were words. Those words could have cost him considerable standing and income. He deliberately spoke them anyway. Courage.

Here are a few instances where courage might be called for, even in our modern, somewhat zombified era:

To say no to your child can risk making him or her mad at you for a time.

To tell the boss that a proposed decision isn't wise can risk being on the outs or considered "not a team player."

To speak up about a public policy can risk friends and relatives disliking you (or even unfriending you on Facebook, as a friend of mine discovered).

To share something about your past, or about struggles you go through, can risk people thinking less of you or even using that knowledge against you.

Yet, as Stephen King marvelously puts it, "There is no gain without risk, perhaps no risk without love."

But How to Actually Do *the Courageous Thing?*

Ay, there's the rub. Some situations can still involve risk in doing something that needs to be done. But how to actually *do* that courageous act? Our fear of negative consequences is always there urging us not to speak or act. We're hard-wired to want acceptance from the group. And the risk of losing a job, or even just one's status within the company, plays on our deep-seated, biological fear of a lack of resources for the future. So in light of these very natural concerns, how can you be brave?

First, you can remember and reflect on others who were brave. What we feed our minds affects our behaviors. You can read stories from your faith, events where a woman or man faces risks but shows courage to accomplish some good. You can also recall people from history who risked greatly for social change or the good of others.

Second, you can think about the importance of the act that is called for. If it's standing firm as a parent, you can consider how important it is for your children to develop into mature, responsible adults. If it's speaking up at work, you can remember that the well-being of the company is important not just to yourself, but to all its employees and the communities it affects. If it's sharing something about yourself, think of the potential benefit to the person you'll open up to. If it's standing by someone in a trying time, consider the importance of your loyalty to him or her.

In other words, focus on the need for the deed. Civil rights leader Cesar Chavez focused on the importance of helping people have decent living conditions: "It is my deepest belief that only by giving life do we find life, that the truest act of courage, the strongest act of manliness is to sacrifice ourselves for others in a totally non-violent struggle for justice. To be a man is to suffer for others. God help us to be men."

Third, you can acknowledge that brave people do feel fear. Mark Twain aptly wrote, "Courage is resistance to fear, mastery of fear – not absence of fear. Except a creature be part coward it is not a compliment to say it is brave." Gen. George Patton admitted candidly that all men feel fear in battle, but courage "is fear holding on a minute longer." Former Navy SEAL Howard Wasdin, commenting on the mission to capture Osama bin Laden said, "The difference between being afraid and a warrior is controlling that fear and using it as a tool in accomplishing the mission."

Finally, you can find others to be brave with. Does it seem to lessen the bravery if the deed is shared? Perhaps it does in our modern minds, formed as they are in our highly individualistic culture. But recall that even the Lone Ranger was far from alone (and many times it was Tonto who really saved the day). The Hebrew patriarch Abraham left Ur to find the Promised Land not alone, but with his extended family. Jesus deliberately set his face towards Jerusalem and crucifixion, in the company of twelve friends. George Washington didn't fight the British without an army. In fact in that conflict, old Ben Franklin remarked, "We must all hang together or assuredly we shall all hang separately." And it was with her friends and colleagues that Alice Paul risked freedom and health for women's suffrage. If the company of others dilutes the bravery, then most of our heroes just got disqualified.

Modern research shows that a social element actually is often an important part of bravery. Social psychologists have investigated why bystanders sometimes look on and do nothing when witnessing an assault, while at other times people will intervene. One important factor for intervening is seeing someone else act first. That first (*very* brave) person shows other potential helpers hanging back that they will have an ally in the fight. This breaks the ice of anonymity and can even transform a crowd of onlookers into a band of helpers. So if you feel a situation calls for bravery, find an ally, and more than one if possible. You will feel more free to be courageous (and your chances for success improve, too). As the Hebrew proverb tells us, "if an attacker prevails against one, two shall withstand him; and a threefold cord is not quickly broken."

Note that it was 1957 in which Louis spoke up about segregation. Conditions were as bad or worse in 1927 or '37, but people speaking up then was far more rare. In the 1950s, however, the Movement was afoot. Many other people, black and white, were speaking up and taking action then. The risks to his career were still just as real as if he had been alone, but the existence of potential allies probably played a part in Pops taking his stand when he did.

Now is a different era, but just as in Louis Armstrong's day, there will be moments that arise in your life where right action risks loss. To echo Cesar Chavez, in those times may you not shrink back as an onlooker, but step forward and act as a true man or woman.

Practices

As discussed earlier, one way to have an inner reserve of courage is to read or view stories of courageous people. Such stories abound in our faith traditions. The book of Esther from the Hebrew scriptures, and Stephen's brave retort to his captors in the seventh chapter of Acts immediately come to mind. Also, the story of the Prophet Muhammad's refusal to give in to demands to renounce Allah shows his willingness to be put to death for his faith.

War, of course, provides ample opportunity for sacrifice and risk. Michael Shaara's great novel, *The Killer Angels*, is the basis of the film *Gettysburg*, both of which have examples of courage in the face of great loss and tragedy. Another story set during war is *Schindler's List*, though Oskar Schindler's courage occurs not on the battlefield, but behind the scenes.

One can also look to people and events from the civil rights and women's movements for examples of bravery. A great children's book with a bit of suspense and a surprise ending is Robert Coles' *The Story of Ruby Bridges*. My high school students were knocked out by the film *Iron Jawed Angels* about Alice Paul, Lucy Burns and their compatriots who were jailed, beaten, and force-fed for daring to picket the White House for the right to vote.

These are all stories that are entertaining and also serve to prime our minds so we will show courage when the time comes.

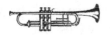

Listening Suggestions

Links to audio and video files are found at
www.livelikelouis.com.

"(What Did I Do to Be So) Black and Blue" is from the Broadway show in which Louis became a breakout star in 1929. Originally the tune was written for a black woman considered too black (as opposed to "browns and yellers") to get a man. Louis altered the lyrics to be more generally about the situation of blacks in an officially racist America. He performed it throughout his career.

"Fables of Faubus" is a piece by Charles Mingus of the next generation of jazz musicians, more outspoken and edgy in their approach to race in America. In this piece, without using words the musicians satirize the racist governor, portraying him as a buffoon. Mockery is often the sharpest put-down. See what you think.

In 1970 Louis recorded the anthem of the civil rights movement, "We Shall Overcome." Many stars and friends, including Tony Bennett and jazz pioneer Miles Davis, were on hand to comprise the backing choir. He quieted them before recording the song, urging them to "sing like you never sang before. This is a beautiful song and it's our song."

9 Body and Soul

*in which Louis shows us
the power of purpose*

When you watch the movie "Hello Dolly," you have to wait almost until the end, during the big production number with its chorus of singing waiters. All of a sudden, there's Satchmo in a wonderful cameo appearance, singing that famous title song with Barbara Streisand. His charm and voice are in full force, though he looks drawn. For by 1968, when the movie was shot, fifty years of constant touring had caught up with him. He went in to see the doctor later that year, was diagnosed with congestive heart failure, and was hospitalized. He told his doctor, Gary Zucker, his life "wasn't worth anything" if he couldn't play his trumpet. After rest and medical treatment, he was released in spring of 1969. For the first time in his life, he became a homebody in Queens. He made reel-to-reel recordings of himself reflecting on his life, created collages on the tape boxes, and wrote more memoirs. Sometimes he would walk around the house with his trumpet in his hands, occasionally blowing into it just a bit, against doctor's orders. Performing on it was out of the question, according to the doctor; but any long-term retirement was out of the question, according to Louis Armstrong.

In 1970 he recorded two albums, just singing. It wasn't enough. In the fall of that year he started playing again, calling the All Stars back into existence for a stint in Vegas and making numerous TV appearances including the one with Johnny Cash mentioned earlier. In March of 1971 Pops took a two-week engagement at New York's Waldorf-Astoria hotel. His doctor thought it would kill him, but after talking with Louis, they compromised: Pops could play if he took a room at the hotel and left it only to go downstairs and perform. To Louis Armstrong, music was life, and he completed what would be his last engagement. What had led Dr. Zucker to compromise was Louis's response when informed the two-week gig might kill him: "Doc, that's all right, I don't care. My whole life, my whole soul, my whole spirit is to blooow that horn."

And It Really Was

Louis Armstrong certainly knew what he was about. Though not the stereotypical, grim workaholic, Louis made it clear throughout his life that music was his priority, mainly through his horn. When people with only a passing familiarity with Louis now hear his name, they'll often respond with a comment about his singing, perhaps even imitating it. Certainly, singing was a big part of his appeal. But in his mind he was a trumpet-playing entertainer on a mission to bring happiness to people. He knew what he was about and he stuck to it, thereby living a life of meaning and purpose.

In New York in the 1920s, it bothered him that his band mates spent their off-duty time drinking and playing cards instead of listening to, and learning from, other musicians. As an evening progressed and his colleagues' liquor took its toll, their sloppy demeanor on the bandstand irked him even more. He was a musical athlete surrounded by teammates not nearly as dedicated as he. "When I pick up that horn, that's all. The world's behind me, and I don't concentrate on nothin' but it. . . . That's my livin' and my life."

And though his fourth marriage was a good one, he made plain his priority: "First comes my horn, and then Lucille. But the horn comes first." This wasn't to disparage the woman he loved for three decades. When Louis said this in the 1950s, he had been supporting himself and others by his trumpet playing for nearly forty years; his immense fame had shown him how important his talent was to the world. His New York Times obituary included a quote that summarizes his life's purpose:

> I never tried to prove nothing, just always wanted to give a good show. My life has been my music, it's always come first, but the music ain't worth nothing if you can't lay it on the public. The main thing is to live for that audience, 'cause what you're there for is to please the people.

The Power of a Purpose

It's clear that Louis Armstrong felt his life had a purpose. Many people feel the same way. As thinking beings who create objects to serve functions, we naturally want to know what purpose *we* were created for. We want to believe that our be-ing is not just an accident or coincidence, and that surviving and passing on genes is not all there is to the game of life. Psychiatrist and Holocaust survivor Victor Frankl called this "man's search for meaning" in his famous book of the same name.

But many people don't feel a purpose to their lives. Unlike most human beings throughout time, many of us in modern society haven't been taught a Truth accepted by everyone around us. There now is not one, standard version of who the god or gods are, what the world is, what our place in it is, or what proper living is. Since our culture lacks one, unquestioned Truth, it instead presents each of us with a number of religions, philosophies, and worldviews from which to choose. This great variety of ideas, each with its ardent believers, has had the effect of leaving many of us adrift with no overarching reason for living. Lacking a purpose for existence, it's easy then to live on autopilot, imitating those around us or taking our cues from advertisers and the mass media. Others do sense something is wrong and incomplete; they feel ill at ease, even empty. "Anomie" is what sociologist Emile Durkheim called this feeling, literally "without a guiding principle." You can find this form of anomie sometimes in retirees (usually men) who lived to work and find nothing to take its place when their career ends. Pastor Rick Warren has certainly tapped into our desire for a sense of meaning and mission, selling 30 million copies of his book, *The Purpose-Driven Life*.

Like Pastor Warren, many people do derive a sense of purpose from their religion. Their reason for existing is usually to serve God and/or do good for others. Some people have even more specific purposes: they exist to support their family or to raise their children to be healthy and compassionate people. Still others live for their career, maybe just to move up a corporate ladder, or to make the world better through a service or product. As behavioral scientists have studied happiness in the last decade or so, they've found one of the key ingredients is this sense of mission, especially being in service to a cause greater than oneself. Lecturer Tal Ben-Shahar taught Harvard's most popular class, Positive Psychology, and he writes, "Happiness lies at the intersection between pleasure and meaning. Whether at work or at home, the goal is to engage in activities that are both personally significant and enjoyable." Researcher Ed Diener has found that "as humans we actually require a sense of meaning to thrive."

One way to feel a sense of purpose and meaning is to consciously state it and keep it in mind. A helpful tool is a personal mission or purpose statement. Now, I know if you were in the business world in the 1990s, the odds are at least fifty-fifty you served (or were forced to serve) on a committee to write a corporate mission statement. It's easy to mock many that were produced that way. Being a sucker for things that sound as if they'll do some good, I helped craft a mission statement both at work and at church. The one at work was typical of the bad ones: too wordy and promptly forgotten. It's too bad, because if people know and believe in an organization's mission, it can certainly help them and the company. Too often, though, the statements were corporate gobbledy-gook, which Scott Adams' *Dilbert* website ably mocked with an online mission statement generator. It cobbled together random words and phrases that unfortunately ended up sounding remarkably like many actual corporate statements: "The purpose of SatchCo is to dynamically interface with multiple vendor inputs, while maximizing integral buy-in, to deliver the most cost-integrated service possible to our end users." Look online and you'll find websites with real-life examples just as incomprehensible, foisted on employees who deserved better.

But a good mission statement – now that really can be beneficial, helping to keep the main thing the main thing. My church's purpose statement was concise and memorable. We used it on bulletins and signs and spoke of it in meetings and worship. Our purpose was to love God and other people, and to help people become followers of Jesus. Maybe some activities would stray from the stated purpose of the group, but at least they could be evaluated in light of our mission, to see if they should continue. The U.S. Army's purpose statement is very concise and gives clear direction to the group. The army exists "to fight and win our nation's wars." I have a personal purpose statement for my career, which I use in my email signature: to help young people gain knowledge and become better thinkers. I'm far from perfect at this, but the words guide me to choose what I have the kids do in class and at home.

Even without an overt mission statement, some people are still very purpose-driven, committed to something larger than just subsisting and buying whatever new things gets marketed at them. Some of the most focused people I know of don't usually have a written statement, but they nevertheless feel an intensely strong sense of purpose: Olympic athletes. Their mission is to place as high as they can in the medal competition, ideally to be standing on the top platform hearing their national anthem ringing out. This purpose guides how they spend nearly every minute of every day, down to every morsel of food and drop of liquid they put in their bodies. Whether it's an image of being on the medal stand, defeating an enemy, or producing better thinkers, having a purpose guides behavior and makes success more likely in any endeavor. As we learned in this book's introduction, beginning with the end in mind is one of Steven Covey's famous seven habits of highly effective people.

A sense of mission can also help you prepare for the future. Although a person might stumble into success occasionally, your chances rise dramatically the better prepared you are. The Allied leaders knew in 1944 their mission was to successfully land a sizable invasion force in France. This clear and simple purpose, closely connected with the larger goal of defeating Germany, guided them in all their months of planning and rehearsing for D-Day. Likewise I've seen a strong sense of purpose (often to become a doctor or dentist) motivate students to study hard for years and years ahead of time. So often, the success we see is the result of considerable hard work done outside of the limelight, all motivated by having a mission in mind.

Louis's sense of purpose led him to live it out through his work. I almost hesitate to call it "work," since that word has the connotation of being unenjoyable or even distasteful, something you *have* to do. True, he earned his living from music, but performing was obviously a joy to Louis. "Do what you love and you'll never work a day in your life," the saying goes. Writer Joseph Campbell advised us to "follow our bliss," and so Satchmo did. Following that bliss and earning his living were one and the same. "Pops loved to play the horn," one of his sidemen observed. "That's what kept him going. If we had two or three days off, he'd get restless and was ready to play again."

Some people assumed longtime manager Joe Glaser was a slave-driver, forcing Louis to play an endless string of one-nighters. Actually, the reverse was true. Louis's friend, cornetist Ruby Braff, recalled the manager actually wanting to carve some time out of his client's performing schedule for other projects. Louis reportedly told Glaser, "You ever give me a night off, go find yourself a new boy." Braff recalled, "Every night was a party for him. For him to have four weeks of no parties was like, 'What are you doing me, a big favor?'" Once,

Louis was somehow convinced to take an eight-week vacation cruise. Rather than lay off the band, Louis's management gave them a paid vacation. Clarinetist Joe Darensbourg recalled just getting into the swing of relaxing beside the swimming pool when the phone rang. The office was calling to cut short his leisure. Louis had gotten bored on the cruise and needed to get back to work playing his trumpet, bringing happiness to his hearers.

Recall how, even when his health was failing him, Louis kept performing, first vocally, then again on trumpet. He kept on doing what he felt he was meant to do, what he *had* to do. So, his life continued to be meaningful. Researchers have shown that continuing to do the things that give us pleasure and meaning reduces stress and lessens depression. Given the precarious state of his health in the early 1970s, his return to performing and living out his purpose probably kept Louis living longer than he would have, in a forced retirement.

Serving a Purpose in a Less-Than-Ideal Job

For any number of reasons, you might not feel "called" to the job you have. You might not even like it, much less love it, as Louis loved playing music. I'm not going to glibly tell you to just change careers, and start doing what you most enjoy. In an ideal world, yes, that would be most preferable. But I'm enough of a realist to know that, for some very important reasons, a career change might not be possible or the best choice. Children need feeding and mortgages need paying. If I felt I had been meant all along to be a professional jazz musician and quit teaching, with its good salary and health benefits, that would certainly be an unloving act toward my family, who depend on me.

If you're a student, however – because of your position near life's starting gate – you likely *are* in a position to discern an occupational calling and answer it. It's not always possible (due to those pesky food and rent bills), but often it is. I highly recommend the bestselling career-choice and self-discovery book, *What Color Is Your Parachute?* There's a good chance you'll get a copy for graduation. Yes, the Dr. Seuss book about the places you'll go has a snazzier cover (and Seuss-ian rhyming), but *Parachute* is really worth reading and doing the activities it provides.

For those seemingly stuck – at least for the time being – in a job you don't love, you still have some options. You can regularly, deliberately think of your job's good qualities. Try doing this during the morning commute, rather than anticipating things that might go wrong as we're so prone to do. What we think about earlier affects how we perceive and respond later. Also, you can give thanks for those positives as you remember them. One of the secrets to happiness is wanting what you have, and giving thanks helps that feeling arise. Furthermore, you can find or develop a mission within your work role. Someone who feels stuck as, say, a landscape worker, could envision a mission to create beauty or bring order out of chaos.

If there is a specific calling you feel, a bliss you

would follow, you can often pursue it as an amateur (Latin for someone who does something "for the love of it"). If I felt that calling to be a musician, but needed to remain a teacher to support my family, I could play jazz on the side. I would occasionally make some dough, and might also volunteer for the local arts center's benefits or play in church or temple. Since doing anything for your living can become a drag, this might in fact be a more blissful way of following it, rather than making music my day job.

Regardless of how you come to it, sensing a purpose, feeling yourself to be on a mission, is the antidote to the zombie-esque life of quiet desperation Thoreau saw most people leading. Knowing and fulfilling a mission at home or work can transform it from drudgery or a necessary evil, into a venue in which to fulfill a purpose and find meaning. Of course you will sometimes wander or become distracted from it; welcome to the human race. But knowing your purpose will inspire you as Louis's did him. It will imbue your thoughts and actions with meaning and power.

Practices

One Specific Calling?

As far as a general purpose for your existence, we'll save that for the final chapter. Let's focus for now on more specific purposes. Louis felt a very specific calling, a "first thing" he kept first all his life: playing the trumpet for people to enjoy. Similarly, some of us live our lives with one specific purpose whether we are aware of it or not. Some live almost exclusively for their children. Others live to achieve higher standing in a community or corporation. Still others live for their job or profession. It's good to acknowledge such a purpose, whether just to make it overt and affirm it, or to examine its worth. See if you can finish the sentence below.

My actions show I live specifically to _____.

If you don't perceive one, specific purpose or mission to your life, rest easy, neither do I. I have many interests and activities. If you do perceive one – especially if you hadn't realized it before – give thought to that purpose and how it can be used for good. Likely it's worthy, but occasionally we can look back and see what we were living for was misguided. Self-examination is never wasted.

Having a Purpose for Each Role

If you (like me) don't feel one, dominant calling like playing the trumpet or being a dental assistant, you still play certain roles in life. Developing and feeling a purpose in these roles will help guide you to perform them more happily and successfully. I mentioned a purpose I have in my teaching. In another area of life, as a father, my purpose is to produce adults who are as capable as they can be, and who contribute positively to other people. Try writing some sentences like the following, for each of your different roles or settings:

As a(n)_____,
my purpose is to _____.

At _____,
my purpose is to _____.

I have my teaching mission posted in two places in my classroom. You might use the ol' sticky-note trick to keep each role's purpose before you. Remembering these purposes will guide your actions so you will keep the main thing the main thing and be more successful.

Listening Suggestions

*Links to audio and video files are found at
www.livelikelouis.com.*

With these tunes, we'll bookend Pops' career. "Just Gone" is the earliest recording of Louis Armstrong. You'll have to listen hard to hear him. He plays the second (lower) cornet part with King Oliver's group in 1923. The story goes that in these early recordings, the studio was very narrow and Louis had to be placed far in the back, his playing was so strong.

At the far end of Louis's life is "Whistle While You Work," from his album of Disney tunes. This is from the last recording session of the last album to feature Pops on trumpet. Plus, it's about enjoying your work, which Louis did with gusto for over fifty years.

An attitude of joy: Pops at work, sharing happiness with his audience at Carnegie Hall, February 1947.

10 What a Wonderful World

*in which Louis reminds us
of our ultimate purpose*

We've encountered Louis in the recording studio several times already. First we saw him dropping some lyrics but going with the flow by scat singing. Then, nearly forty years later, we witnessed him recording an obscure show tune that became a monster hit. "Hello Dolly" was so huge, in fact, Pops then made a number of similar recordings of Broadway songs done his way. Now we meet him in 1967 about to record a song that will wonderfully deviate from that formula.

Sometimes we look back on the sixties through little, round, rose-colored glasses. Before studying the period, my students often picture a carefree time of sun-dappled hippies dancing in a park, arms upraised and eyes blissfully shut. Certainly there was a spirit of opportunity and positive change in the air. Just as certainly, though, there was strife and hatred: shocking assassinations, riots, vitriolic resistance to the civil rights movement, and the endless jungle warfare that was Vietnam.

Record producer Bob Thiele set out to write a song to counter all the bad nightly news. He wanted to emphasize "the love and sharing people make possible for themselves and each other every day." His song, "What a Wonderful World," spoke of simple things: trees, clouds, babies, growth. It spoke of the natural rhythm of day and night, and of the bond of brotherly love among friends. Since he had earlier produced an album for Louis, Thiele knew his song matched well with the entertainer's outlook on life and that he was just the right person to sing it. He made a demonstration record of the tune and visited Louis on the road. While the demo was still playing, Louis interrupted with the name he used for all his friends: "Pops, I dig it. Let's do it."

Louis had no long-term contract with any record label, so they went to Thiele's label, ABC-Paramount Records. Because of the extra cost to hire an orchestra, Louis accepted the minimum pay allowed by the musicians' union, only about $250. The head of the label, Larry Newton, sat in the control room. But he couldn't abide the fact that his label wasn't recording another up-tempo Satchmo romp like "Dolly." As the session went on, he became more and more upset. Why abandon a formula that worked, and was liable to make more (possibly much more) money than this sappy ballad? Newton got madder and madder at what he saw as a missed opportunity for profit. He reached a breaking point and proclaimed the session over. He would send all the musicians home and scrap the whole thing, basically "firing" the legendary

Louis Armstrong. Thiele, much to his credit, coura-
geously ordered the company president out of the
control room. As we know, the record was finished,
the world responded to its message of hope, and it
became a big, wonderful hit.

In England. There the record was number one
with a bullet, as Casey Kasem used to say, selling
over half a million copies. But not in America. Newton wouldn't allow his company to promote the record. Louis performed it on the *The Tonight Show*
and in concert, but the recording remained essentially unknown in the States until 1987. The song
finally found its deserved fame in America through
its use in the film *Good Morning, Vietnam.* The song
plays ironically underneath scenes of bombing and
destruction, some of the strife Thiele wanted to
counter. Still, the positive song struck a chord with
Americans. Two decades after its initial release,
"Wonderful World" was re-issued as a single,
earned a spot in the Top 40, and was eventually selected for the Grammy Hall of Fame in 1999. Now
any Armstrong compilation CD is incomplete without it. Rather than being best known for a (very
fine) ditty about a Dolly, Louis is most remembered
for a song about friendship, love, and appreciating
the simple things of life.

Although jazz critics might prefer Louis to be
best known for one of his trumpet masterpieces,
could there be any song that better matches the
man? While researching this book, I was struck by
the positivity of Louis's language, how often he fla-
vored his speech and writing with words like
"beautiful," "wonderful," and "lovely." When

Louis introduced older tunes, he felt compelled to praise them twice in one sentence, announcing, "Now for one of those good ol' good ones . . ." We've seen earlier how he saw beyond the flaws of lesser musicians, focusing on the good they had to offer. And when he remembered his upbringing in New Orleans among poverty and crime, he would often speak of it in kind or even humorous terms, accentuating the positive. As legendary record producer George Avakian remarked, Satchmo's ever-present smile was no act, but "a smile that came from within, all the way. He took everything that came his way and he turned it into an asset no matter what happened to him."

Two thousand years ago, my favorite rabbi put it this way: "The eye is the lamp for the body; if your eye be healthy, your whole body will be full of light." In other words, the more positively we see the world, the more positive world we'll be living in. One day, for example, I listened to a positive speaker urge me (via an ancient technology known as "cassette") to say to myself, "Something good is gonna happen to me today." Throughout the day I had taken her advice and repeated those words. That night, I was reading near a window. I noticed a very bright light coming from over my shoulder. I turned and looked outside. No, not an angel! It was the moon shining very brightly. Now, on a normal night I would've just turned back around (or even grumped about the glare); but that night, thanks to the earlier priming of my mind, I noticed how beautiful the moon was. A good thing happened to me simply because I had the eyes to see it as good.

Viewing things as positive is the quickest way to have more positive things happen to you.

Someone else with Louis's upbringing and the grueling decades he spent on the road might have looked back bitterly. But because of his outlook, for Louis those same circumstances could prompt him to remark near the end, "I think I've had a beautiful life." And so he did. Because Louis saw good, he thus was full of light and able to share it back to the world. Looking back, Pops wrote, "My whole life has been happiness. Through all of the misfortunes, etc., I did not plan anything. Life was there for me and I accepted it. And life, whatever came out, has been beautiful to me, and I love everybody."

Our Great Purpose

Let us return to Larry Newton, the executive who wanted to stop the recording session. Please remember, as Pops would, that he had some good qualities. We know this because he was a human being and we all have some. I'm sorry the story presents him as kind of a villain. After all, his job was to maximize shareholder value. Yet, you can't help but see a contrast between Newton, concerned about money and wanting to see a record fail; and Louis, wanting to get out of a rut and give people a song of hope and joy. Through this contrast we see Louis's larger purpose, which he lived throughout his life. We spoke last chapter of Louis's living to play his trumpet. He spoke of that purpose many times, as we've seen. But in a comment he made about his audiences, you can hear that even the horn was a means to a larger end: "People love me and my music and you know I love them. The minute I walk on the bandstand, they know they're going to get something good. I see to that."

All through his life, through his music and through his person, Louis lived to contribute to the good of others.

This is not to say he was perfect. Like Larry Newton and you and me, being human he was also flawed. Nevertheless, with his music he brought joy to millions. In his personal life, he deliberately treated people with kindness and generosity. Throughout his life, starting as a boy supporting his family, to old age, checking with neighborhood kids about their homework, Louis was a *contributor*.

Maybe this seems an odd or cold word to describe the outgoing Louis Armstrong. I used to dislike the word, myself, when people would speak of wanting to raise children to become "contributing members of society." It seemed bland, like producing unthinking cogs for the machine. But upon reflection, a "contributor" implies activity, as opposed to a passive cog just spinning in place. A contributor adds to the well-being and well-functioning of another person, a family, a community, an organization. A contributor applies thought, word, and deed toward some good end: easing pain, encouraging joy, helping someone grow. Now I think being a contributor is *precisely* what I want for my own children, according to their different talents and personalities.

We noted in an earlier chapter how it's natural

to focus on negatives. However, it's also natural to cooperate and contribute. As social animals we inherit the urge to help others. In our pre-history, individuals who helped those they lived with raise their kids, hunt food, or defend the cave, would be helped in turn by those same comrades, thus passing on genes for an inclination to cooperate. "Together Everyone Achieves More," the sports adage goes. This survival advantage to helping others is probably why we get that reward of a warm feeling when we help someone in need, and why spending twenty dollars on another person "leads to greater boosts in happiness than spending that money on oneself." True, we're hardwired to compete and care about ourselves, but we're also hardwired to care about and contribute to the good of other people. Caring for others is so common – and having truly no empathy is so rare – we even have labels for people who are purely selfish: "psychopaths" or "sociopaths."

Caring for others and seeking their good is bred deep in the bone, etched into our being long before we were even *Homo sapiens*. In an experiment in 1964, researchers found that rhesus monkeys would refuse to pull a chain that gave them food when it also gave a shocking jolt of electricity to a fellow monkey. One went almost two weeks without food, to keep another from feeling pain. Famed primatologist Frans de Waal remarks, "Those primates were literally starving themselves" to help others. Numerous observations and studies have shown how chimps, our nearest relatives, live and work together, kiss to make up, even console each other after a loss by putting an arm around the other's shoulder.

In addition to a biological urge to do good, many religions teach that being oriented toward our fellow human beings is also morally right. The Hebrew scriptures include many provisions for participating positively in the lives of others, from shared rituals to leaving the edges of farm fields unharvested, so the poor and foreigners might "glean" some food for themselves. The book of Leviticus instructs its readers to "love your neighbor as yourself," later quoted by Jesus of Nazareth when asked to name the greatest commandment of all. Of course much of his teaching, and the rest of the New Testament, exhorts his followers to live lovingly by helping others and participating in the shared life known as "the body of Christ." Charitable giving is so important to Islam it is one of its five pillars. Other religions, too, teach that we should live out a love for God by caring for other people and contributing to the greater good. The Dalai Lama says, "My religion is very simple. My religion is kindness."

For those of us in the fast-growing classification "spiritual but not religious," we can deduce this grand purpose to life not from a religious book or teachings, but from the unfolding story of the universe. It is a story of small, simple wholes that, over time, come together, collaborate, and cooperate into larger wholes. *These* wholes, in turn, combine with similar units into another, more complex whole with its own emergent properties. Which then cooperates with others into a new, larger thing, and so on, and so on: energy to matter to subatomics to atoms to molecules to substances to cells to tissues to organs to organisms to communities to societies to . . . ?

Some thinkers even describe the universe itself as being conscious now. That sounds pretty "out there." But we say that "you" are conscious, even though only part of you really performs that function. So the cosmos itself can likewise be considered conscious, since *it* has a thinking part (us). Moreover, just as the cells and organs in your body combine and cooperate to produce a healthy you, so individual humans all over the planet have been combining and collaborating in fits and starts for thousands of years to become healthy families, communities, and societies. Now many of us are participating, especially through trade and the internet, in a new, emerging whole. A species in which a large number of members truly combine their thoughts and cultures is a new thing, a social organism made up of individual human beings, but having properties all its own. And through reason, creativity, and free will, we can influence how We/It develops. The eminent futurist Barbara Marx Hubbard calls this "conscious evolution."

Thus we can deliberately take our place in this ongoing development, contributing and collaborating, helping others who in turn will add to the emerging Us. Is this morally imperative? Stephen Tramel, a wonderful philosophy professor, warned us that you can't get an "ought" from an "is." That is, just because the universe is a great chain of ever-developing collaboration, it's a bad leap of logic to say people *ought* – are morally obligated – to live likewise. Nevertheless, cooperating and contributing is living in right relationship with the *Logos*, the underlying order and creative principle of the cosmos. To this observer (and many others) it just seems right to live in harmony with the ongoing direction of the universe.

So, you can arrive at positive, proactive living as the purpose for your existence from either of two starting points. From the pathway of traditional religion, it's a response to God, to whom you're grateful, and who desires this of you. It is healthy, whole living as God has designed for you. Coming from a scientific, evolutionary understanding, a life based on contributing and collaborating is in accord with the progression of all things, singing in tune with the Music of the Spheres, a composition in development for fourteen billion years and counting. The good news is, regardless of your starting point, this way lies true and meaningful life.

How Louis Contributed

Louis lived life for the benefit of others. Foremost was the joy he gave back through his glorious trumpeting and soulful singing. His comments from that period describe the higher purpose he and his music achieved with his audiences.

> They get their soul lifted because they got the same soul I have the minute I hit a note.
> . . . I love my audience and they love me and

we just have one good time whenever I get
up on the stage – it's such a lovely pleasure.

People responded to Louis's gift of happiness with
such enthusiasm all over the world, he was nick-
named "Ambassador Satch" in the 1950s. To borrow from Jesus's words again, Louis not only returned to the world the light his healthy eyes saw,
he received it back again in good measure, pressed
down, shaken together, and running over.

Louis Armstrong found his niche in the great
endeavor of adding to the good. His was to use music to share love and joy with his hearers; he even
described himself as being "in the service of happiness." But as important as happiness is, it's only one
way to build up or bless others. Another person,
quiet and good at numbers, will find a different
way to contribute. A serious person who likes making things in wood will find yet another. A boister-
ous soul in the business world, still another.

Betty Erni finds her place to contribute in the
pressbox elevator of Ford Field, home of the Detroit
Lions. Columnist Michael Rosenberg calls this elevator operator "the most openly happy person I
have ever met." In her elevator Betty is uncon-
cerned that she's unable to watch the game on Sun-
days (perhaps part of the secret of her happiness).
"I'm too busy thinking: Who is going to get on my
elevator that I can bless?" Whatever your personality and talents, you too have family members, co-
workers, neighbors, and strangers you interact
with: people who get on your elevator, so to speak,
all of whom you can intend well-being toward, and

try to bless. The important thing is to be about the work of contributing however you're able.

Louis spread love in many avenues of life. He adopted his cousin's son when he himself was just a teen. He was very generous, giving away thousands of dollars a year in cash, "greasing the mitts" of people who came to his dressing room, and sending monthly envelopes to old friends in need. In his old age Louis and Lucille would invite the neighborhood kids in to watch TV and have ice cream. His overall positive demeanor uplifted those around him; he was one of those people who make you feel better just by entering a room. George Avakian said, "He was the finest person that I ever knew among all the artists I worked with. I mean that as a human being. He was a terrific guy, just as genuine as can be, and he was a gentleman in every respect, treated people very, very well. He was a – he's just one of the finest people I ever met in my life."

Louis knew the great purpose of blessing and contributing. Maybe it was in his DNA to see the good and be positive. Or, maybe he absorbed it by watching the way his mother or granny acted. Maybe both. And maybe you've known a few such people like Louis, folks for whom very positive thinking and living seem to be as easy as breathing.

To others of us (including your author), positivity doesn't come so naturally. We often find ourselves eating, breathing, working, and recreating without much thought about it or, worse, focusing on the negatives. We who are like that need to keep our Great Purpose more consciously in mind. We need to be reminded of our higher calling so we'll find ways to live it out, even if that just means viewing what we're already doing through the lens of contributing to others.

Fortunately, there are people to help us be mindful of our common calling to contribute and build others up. That's the purpose of this chapter, and of entire books by inspiring authors far more skilled than I. There are websites and daily email services built to remind us of life's deeper truth. And, as noted above, living for others is a focus of all the great faiths, which have preachers, teachers, musicians, and writers to inspire us. Last and not least are the ordinary people who, in their approach to life, are actually extra-ordinary: the friends, co-workers, and associates close at hand who are especially loving and positive, people we can be with and emulate.

The subtitle of this book makes an implied promise that living like Louis will help you lead a better life. Truth be told, the point of living isn't just to have yourself a wonderful life. It's to help create a more wonderful world. Late in Louis's life, in the midst of personally answering hundreds of fan letters, his secretary asked how he handled all the love sent his way. Louis admitted it could occasionally get heavy. In five words, though, he summarized his approach to life and his response to people's outpouring of love:

"I give it right back."

Let us go and do likewise.

Practices

Eye Care

We heard earlier that a healthy eye sees the good and fills your whole body with light. More concretely, as we see good and intend good, we actually influence other people to act more positively. This is thanks to some brain cells we all have called mirror neurons. You've experienced this many times, often without even knowing. If someone seems nervous, you'll probably get a bit nervous too, and respond guardedly. If someone seems aggressive, right away you will be too, at least a little bit. On the other hand, if you approach someone openly and positively, he or she will usually mirror that and be more prone to treat you well in return, creating a positive feedback loop.

But what if you're not naturally positive? As we noted in chapter six, there's a strong survival instinct to attend to negatives and want to fix them. How can you come to look on things more positively? This is the focus of many books including Martin Seligman's bestseller, *Learned Optimism*. It's also a common focus of cognitive therapy, which involves having people identify where their thinking is unhelpful, then learning and practicing new scripts to say internally when reacting or reflecting.

Like many worthwhile endeavors (including the road to Carnegie Hall), common to all approaches is practice. Here are a few specifics to try:

List your blessings in writing every morning, or some other regular time. Maybe in the business world, lunch time would be especially helpful, to re-set your mind after a stressful morning. Remember to name things whose goodness is because of their absence, for instance, "I don't have a cold anymore."

You can also list some people or things you often feel negative toward and try to write something positive about them. Again, this is not to deny that sometimes there are certainly problems that need dealing with. However, viewing a challenge differently might help you engage it more proactively.

Many people speak or write out affirmations daily. Try the site *Vital Affirmations* (found at www.vitalaffirmations.com) for some good ones to recite. My favorite? "Life is a joy filled with delightful surprises."

Finally, praying daily for others – aside from the good it might do them directly – certainly will help you be more care-full toward them and toward people in general.

Remembering Your Great Purpose

Years ago I was given the high honor of addressing three hundred graduating high school students at their commencement ceremony. Rather than tell them what to do, I shared and elaborated on a phrase I had recently heard, the Truth I hope you sensed at the heart of this final chapter:

True living comes only through giving.

Of course, "giving" here means more than money, though our materialistic culture has trained us to think of that immediately. There is a famous trinity of T's involved in giving: time, talent, and, yes, treasure. This holistic understanding of giving is just another way of saying what we've called "contributing": putting energy into helping, healing, and building up. As the phrase often attributed to Winston Churchill goes, "We make a living by what we get. We make a life by what we give." Although he didn't actually say that, what he did say is just as inspiring:

> What is the use of living, if it be not to strive for noble causes and to make this muddled world a better place for those who will live in it after we are gone? How else can we put ourselves in harmonious relation with the great verities and consolations of the infinite and the eternal?

To keep this high calling in mind, one way is to associate with others who do. If not in person, you can commune with such people through reading and listening to their words.

Another way to remember our great purpose is by deliberately calling it to mind on a regular basis. In chapter four I offered a simple guided relaxation technique involving simple thoughts coordinated with breathing. As a means of remembering and putting into practice our great mission, here's another one, focusing on the truth of giving and living. As before, sit comfortably in a quiet room. Notice your breathing. Let your mind be as relaxed as you can. Do nothing for about three breaths.

After that, each time you inhale, think,
"True living . . ."

As you exhale, think,
". . . comes only through giving."

Breathe at whatever tempo feels natural; your body will do what's right for you. Continue this for a minute. Repeat as needed. Again, when your mind wanders, gently bring it back to focus on the task at hand with no self-reproach. Feel free to increase the duration if you continue on with this type of meditation, what Christianity calls "breath prayer."

Let me admit here at the end of our last section on practices that I am a pretty normal American: I often forget or neglect to do what's good for me. In fact, as I write this there is a neglected bottle of men's vitamins calling to me from the back of the cupboard. Old habits and the tyranny of the urgent die hard. But when I do remember to practice what has been offered in these sections, I feel better and am a better person. I believe the same will be true for you.

Be well.

Listening Suggestions

Links to audio and video files are found at
www.livelikelouis.com.

Pops was the first jazz musician to record "When the Saints Go Marchin' In." He performed the joyful, rollicking tune countless times with the All Stars. The phrase, "Oh how I want to be in that number," originally referred to the number of people ("saints") who would be allowed to march into heaven. The New Testament Greek word for "saint" is *hagios*, meaning "set aside for a special purpose." In this way, we can think of saints not in a "holier-than-thou" way, but as people meant for the very important purpose of contributing to the good and building others up. Oh, how I want to be in that number. I bet you do too.

In 1970 some of Pops' friends put some new lyrics to the old tune, and re-titled it "Boy From New Orleans." In this version, Louis sings you through his whole life's story. Near the end, the music slows, and Pops offers a very touching, spoken verse that summarizes his lifelong positive outlook and gratitude. I'll leave it unprinted here, since it would have about ten percent of the impact it will have when you hear him say it to you. Historian Ricky Riccardi has pointed out that Pops closed his last shows with this tune, so these words of thanks would have been the last words ever spoken by

Louis onstage. A consummate entertainer and one of humanity's great souls, the boy from New Orleans exited perfectly on a high note of love.

Coda

in which we part, with Louis's blessing

Coda means "tail," and in music the coda is the ending of the piece, when you can tell the musicians are wrapping things up. For instance on "Hello, Dolly," it's when Pops sings, "Dolly – never go away" three times and the musicians finish it off together. So now, O reader, we're at the coda of our exploration of stories from the life of Louis Armstrong. Certainly he had his flaws too, but I've left those to the several thorough biographies you'll find listed in the reading suggestions at the back of this book. This was not to hide anything, but to keep to my double purpose: to encourage and inspire. Any success in those endeavors is due to the terrific person I had the privilege of sharing with you.

We began at the end, with Louis's accomplishments and fame as a way to see how far he traveled. We saw that he transcended a poor, crime-ridden neighborhood and broken family, not letting his circumstances define him. We met two important figures from early in Louis's career, whose encour-

agement was instrumental in his becoming the musician and person he was. We learned of his being
open to different types of people and music, and
being able to roll with unexpected changes. We
were reminded to enjoy our talents and focus on
our strengths, just as Louis was utterly confident of
the high C's he kept in his pocket. We heard the
story of Lucille surprising Pops with a home, and
how much he treasured it and his neighborhood in
Queens. Louis's odd devotion to an intense laxative
reminded us to indulge our own idiosyncrasies, not
being afraid to be ourselves. We heard Louis's stern
rebukes against injustice, words that put his re-
warding career in jeopardy.

Finally, we learned that Louis knew his life's
purpose was to share happiness by playing the
trumpet; and how this was part of an overall life of
sharing joy and contributing to others' well-being.
From a spoken introduction to a version of "What a
Wonderful World" recorded the year before his
death, Louis Armstrong gives us this benediction:

> *And all I'm saying is*
> *see what a wonderful world it would be*
> *if only we'd give it a chance.*
> *Love, baby, love.*
> *That's the secret . . . yeeaah.*

Acknowledgements

I am very grateful to the following people:

My wife, Jane, for her love, encouragement, forbearance, and proofreading skills.

My editor, Tammy Wiles, for her validation, and skill in perceiving many things I could not.

My father, Gerald R. Lynch, for his encouragement and example of work.

My high school band teacher, Grant Hoemke, who taught us you get out of something as much as you put in; and sparked my love of jazz.

Author and archivist Ricky Riccardi, for his encouragement and help.

Author Jen Brady, for her publishing advice.

Jay Brodersen of Archtop Productions, for his encouragement and example of attempting and completing a large undertaking.

Lauren Beversluis, Lynn Thomas, and Peggy Schumann, for their early enthusiasm.

Michael Shulman of Magnum Photos, for facilitating the use of the cover photo.

Author and radio host John St. Augustine, for inspiring me and giving advice.

Authors Dan Schawbel and Roger C. Parker, for unknowingly prompting me to write a book.

The staff of Book World, for market research.

Many friends and colleagues, for encouragement and feedback online.

Suggestions for Further Reading

For a thorough exploration of Louis's life, either of these biographies is a great place to start:

Giddins, Gary. *Satchmo: The Genius of Louis Armstrong.* Boston: Da Capo Press, 2001.

> *This is a terrific, short bio by Gary Giddins, perhaps our finest living jazz writer. The 2001 paperback is fine, but if you can get your hands on the large-format 1988 version (New York: Doubleday), it's* **full** *of rare pictures. It was the companion volume to Giddins' award-winning documentary,* Satchmo, *available on DVD.*

Teachout, Terry. *Pops.* Boston: Houghton Mifflin Harcourt, 2009.

> *Of the longer biographies, this is the one to read, though Bergreen's (see notes) is also good. Teachout, drama critic for the* Wall Street Journal, *is an excellent writer and explores Louis's life completely and sympathetically.*

If you wish to go deeper, try any of these:

Armstrong, Louis. *Louis Armstrong in His Own Words.* Edited by Thomas Brothers. Oxford: Oxford University Press, 1999.

_____. *Satchmo: My Life in New Orleans*. New York: Prentice-Hall, 1954.

Brothers has done yeoman's work assembling a very interesting collection of essays and memoirs – some previously unpublished – written by the Man himself. Pops could write. You'll really get a feel for New Orleans in the early 1900s from Louis's vivid memoirs.

Brower, Stephen. *Satchmo: The Wonderful World and Art of Louis Armstrong*. New York: Abrams, 2009.

Brower has produced a beautiful coffee-table book of Louis's tape-box collages and photos.

Riccardi, Ricky. *The Wonderful World of Louis Armstrong* (website), http://dippermouth.blogspot.com

_____. *What a Wonderful World: The Magic of Louis Armstrong's Later Years*. New York: Pantheon, 2011.

Riccardi is a jazz historian with an encyclopedic knowledge of all things Pops. It's an understatement to call his website a blog: each entry is article-length, usually focusing on a particular song or recording session, with copious info about various versions and takes. Entries include embedded audio and/or video too. His book is exactly what the subtitle promises: with many interesting anecdotes and details, Ric-

cardi thoroughly chronicles Louis's last twenty-five
years. He gracefully refutes the too-widely-held no-
tion that Pops had nothing new to offer after 1950.

Notes & Photo Credits

Below are citations of specific sources. Information or quotations widely available are not cited.

Epigraph

Bach said: Richard Brookhiser, *Right Time, Right Place: Coming of Age with William F. Buckley Jr. and the Conservative Movement* (New York: Basic Books, 2009), 174.

Intro

"Armstrong is to music": "Louis Armstrong Quotes and Tributes," *Satchmo.com,* http://www.satchmo.com/louisarmstrong/quotes.html (accessed September 2009).

"America's Bach": Gary Giddins, *Satchmo: the Genius of Louis Armstrong* (Boston: Da Capo Press, 2001), xiii.

"The bottom line": Reinhold Wagnleitner, ed., *Satchmo Meets Amadeus* (Innsbruck: StudienVerlag, 2007), 30.

"Armstrong practically invented": Andrew Dansby, "Heading Towards Centennial, Louis Armstrong Stands Tall," *Rolling Stone,* August 23, 2000.

"Armstrong influenced Billie Holiday": Jerry Tallmer, "Profile: Tony Bennett," *Thrive NYC,* October 2005, http://www.nycplus.com/nycp6/tonybennett.html (accessed July 2012).

"Do you realize": Giddins, *Satchmo,* xii.

"Without him, no me": Geoffrey C. Ward and Ken Burns, *Jazz: An Illustrated History* (New York: Alfred A. Knopf, 2000), 451.

"You can't play anything": "Louis Armstrong Quotes and Tributes."

1 Don't Fence Me In

Details of Louis's departure are found in Louis Armstrong, *Satchmo: My Life in New Orleans* (New York: Prentice-Hall, 1954; repr., Boston: Da Capo Press, 1986), chap. 1.

Poor but "clean": Laurence Bergreen, *Louis Armstrong: An Extravagant Life* (New York: Broadway Books, 1997), 84.

All types treated: Armstrong, *Satchmo*, 8-9.

On Saturday mornings: Richard Merryman, "An Interview with Louis Armstrong," *Life*, April 15, 1960, 102.

Some fascinating research: Jay Dixit, "Logos: Branded for Life," *Psychology Today*, June 2008, 28.

"I never did want": Ward and Burns, *Jazz*, 124.

"noble human behavior": Wayne Shorter, preface to Michelle Mercer, *Footprints: The Life and Work of Wayne Shorter* (New York: Tarcher/Penguin, 2004), xii.

"Every situation": Deepak Chopra, *Twitter* post, https://twitter.com/deepakchopra, September 17, 2009, 10:34 a.m.

"Every time": Bergreen, *An Extravagant Life*, 6.

2 Keep the Rhythm Going

Details of Louis Armstrong's time at the Colored Waif's Home are found in Louis Armstrong, *Satchmo: My Life in New Orleans*, chap. 3.

"Go get him": Ibid., 34.

"feel good inside; Gee, what a feeling": Ibid., 40.

"Mr. Davis nodded": Ibid., 42.

"I was in": Ibid., 46.

"Louis, I am going": Ibid.

"The way I see it": Louis Armstrong, "Joe Oliver Is Still King," in *Louis Armstrong in His Own Words*, ed. Thomas Brothers (Oxford: Oxford University Press, 1999), 38.

"When he played; had a heart": Louis Armstrong, "Scanning the History of Jazz," in *Louis Armstrong in His Own Words*, 174.

"guarded with his life": Armstrong, *Satchmo*, 100.

"I shall never forget": Louis Armstrong, "The Goffin Notebooks," in *Louis Armstrong in His Own Words*, 85.

The dueling bandwagons story is found in Armstrong, *Satchmo*, 98-99.

"I could go into; I had made up": Ibid., 226.

Details of Louis's departure from New Orleans and reception in Chicago are found in Armstrong, *Satchmo*, chap. 14.

"I can never stop loving": Ibid., 100-101.

"Encouragement is the most": Linda Albert, *Cooperative Discipline* (Circle Pines, MN: American Guidance Service, 1996), 15.

A team of sports science researchers: Joseph L. Andreacci, Linda M. Lemura, Steven L. Cohen, Ethan A. Urbansky, Sara A. Chelland, and Serge P. von Duvillard, "The Effects of Frequency of Encouragement on Performance During Maximal Exercise Testing," *Journal of Sports Sciences* 20, no. 4 (April 2002): 345-352.

Gary Giddins says: Peter Gerler, "The Dozens: King Oliver," *Jazz.com*, http://www.jazz.com/dozens/the-dozens-king-oliver (accessed June 2010).

3 I Get Ideas

Details of Louis Armstrong's experiences with the Karnofskys are found in Louis Armstrong, "Louis Armstrong + the Jewish Family in New Orleans, LA., the Year of 1907," in *Louis Armstrong in His Own Words*, chap. 1.

"The Karnofsky family kept": Ibid., 15-16.

"They were always warm": Ibid., 9.

"I will love": Ibid., 11.

"The best Friend": Ibid., 6.

"He was the least prejudiced musician": George Bornstein, "Satchmo on St. Pat's Day," *Detroit News*, March 17, 2011, 2B.

"White audiences,": Ibid., 11.

Pops was so moved: Jay Smith and Len Guttridge, *Jack Teagarden: The Story of a Jazz Maverick* (Boston: Da Capo Press, 1988), 75.

"Those people who make": Terry Teachout, *Pops* (Boston: Houghton Mifflin Harcourt, 2009), 16.

"Let me tell you something": Bornstein, "Satchmo on St. Pat's Day."

Biographer Terry Teachout believes: Teachout, *Pops*, 144.

1200-item record collection: Michael Cogswell, *Satchmo: The Offstage Story of Louis Armstrong* (Portland, OR: Collectors Press, 2003), 90; Teachout, *Pops*, 291.

In 1968: Teachout, *Pops*, 355.

"Give this son of a gun": Ibid., 281.

recent research: "Speaking Two Languages May Delay Alzheimer's," *NBC News*, http://www.msnbc.msn.com/id/41670925/ns/health-alzheimers_disease/t/speaking-two-languages-may-delay-alzheimers (accessed July 2012).

"It was the Jewish family": Armstrong, "Louis Armstrong + the Jewish Family," 18.

4 Now You Has Jazz

"I dropped the paper": Louis Armstrong, "Jazz on a High Note," *Esquire* 36 (Dec. 1951): 85; quoted in Daniel Stein, *Music Is My Life: Louis Armstrong, Autobiography, and American Jazz* (Ann Arbor: University of Michigan Press, 2012), 62.

a helpful online resource: "The Road to Resilience," *American Psychological Association*, http://www.apa.org/helpcenter/road-resilience.aspx/ (accessed July 2012).

Breathing in, I calm my body: Thich Nhat Hanh, *The Blooming of a Lotus* (Boston: Beacon Press, 1993), 15.

5 Swing That Music

"Come by starting date": Teachout, *Pops*, 87.

"I had it in my pocket": Ward and Burns, *Jazz*, 134.

"shouldy approach to life": David Burns, *The Feeling Good Handbook*, revised ed. (New York: Plume, 1999), 10.

Even among our youth: Sadie F. Dingfelder, "Reflecting on Narcissism: Are Young People More Self-Obsessed Than Ever Before?" *Monitor on Psychology*, www.apa.org/monitor/2011/02/narcissism.aspx (accessed August 2011).

doom loop: Jim Collins, *Good to Great: Why Some Companies Make the Leap and Others Don't* (New York: HarperCollins, 2011), chap. 8.

He likened his philosophy: Louis Armstrong, "Scanning the History of Jazz," in *Louis Armstrong in His Own Words*, 175.

"The clarion call": Gunther Schuller, *Early Jazz* (Oxford: Oxford University Press, 1968), 89.

"If you take": Ricky Riccardi, "75 Years of Louis Armstrong's Unbelievable May 18, 1936, Decca Session," *The Wonderful World of Louis Armstrong*, http://dippermouth.blogspot

.com/2011/05/75-years-of-louis-armstrongs.html (accessed August 2011).

6 *That's My Home*

"Lucille, I might as well": Giddins, *Satchmo*, 115.
"He took one look": Nat Hentoff, *The Jazz Life* (New York: Dial Press, 1961; repr., Boston: Da Capo Press, 1975), 26-27.
"One look at that": Louis Armstrong, "Early Years with Lucille," in *Louis Armstrong in his Own Words*, 144.
650 reel to reel tapes: Many photos of Louis's tape-box collages are found in the marvelous coffee table book, Steven Brower's *Satchmo: The Wonderful World and Art of Louis Armstrong* (New York: Abrams, 2009).
"I love my wife": Louis Armstrong, "Letter to Joe Glaser," in *Louis Armstrong in his Own Words*, 158.
Louis wrote in 1970: Louis Armstrong, "Our Neighborhood," in *Louis Armstrong in his Own Words*, 176-177.
"During my 54 years": Louis Armstrong, "Open Letter to Fans," in *Louis Armstrong in his Own Words*, 183.
Close friend Phoebe Jacobs: Ward and Burns, *Jazz*, 450.
"We don't need": Charles L. Sanders, "Louis Armstrong: The Reluctant Millionaire," *Ebony*, Nov. 1964, 138.
"We've both seen three": Ibid.
a very touching photograph: Ward and Burns, *Jazz*, 452.
"I listened not so much": Ward and Burns, *Jazz*, 316.

7 *It's a Most Unusual Day*

"The food that you all eat": Giddins, *Satchmo*, 30-31.
"one of my toughest customers": Louis Armstrong, "Open Letter to Fans," *Louis Armstrong in His Own Words*, 181.
"I take my Swiss Kriss": Max Jones & John Chilton, *Louis: The Louis Armstrong Story*, 1900-1971 (London: Studio Vista, 1971; repr., Boston: Da Capo Press, 1988), 220.
"Your first dose": Louis Armstrong, "Lose Weight the Satchmo Way," in Bergreen, *An Extravagant Life*, 448-449.
Tony Bennett enjoys: Tony Bennett, in Gary Giddins, *Satchmo*, documentary film, Toby Byron Multiprizes, 1989.
a discussion thread: "Trek T-shirts," *TrekBBS.com*, http://trekbbs

.com/showthread.php?t=99245&highlight=t-shirt (accessed October 2009).

Swiss Kriss Directions: Liberty Hall Jazz Quartet, http://www .libertyhall.com/Stamp/kriss.html (accessed July 2012).

8 Black and Blue

"They wouldn't give up": Louis Armstrong, "Louis Armstrong + the Jewish Family in New Orleans, LA. the Year of 1907," in *Louis Armstrong in His Own Words,* 17.

"I ain't goin' back": "Unconstitutional Law Nixes Satchmo's Mixed Band," *Jet,* Nov. 26, 1959, 56-59.

"There was something": Teachout, *Pops,* 322.

Mr. Armstrong said: Associated Press, "Louis Armstrong, Barring Soviet Tour, Denounces Eisenhower and Gov. Faubus," *New York Times,* September 19, 1957.

We now know; Reaction was mixed: Teachout, *Pops,* 331-332.

Columnist Jim Bishop: Bergreen, *An Extravagant Life,* 318.

Mr. President: Louis Armstrong, Telegram to Dwight D. Eisenhower, Sept. 24, 1957, in *Louis Armstrong in His Own Words,* 194.

"When I see": Brothers, ed., *Louis Armstrong in His Own Words,* 194.

In a wonderful essay: Chuck Klosterman, "My Zombie, Myself: Why Modern Life Feels Rather Undead," *New York Times,* December 3, 2010.

Former Navy SEAL: David Martin, "The Secret SEAL Team That Took Down bin Ladn," *CBS News,* http://www.cbsnews .com/stories/2011/05/06/eveningnews/main20060615 .shtml (accessed May 2011).

One important factor: Wendy Wood, Sharon Lundgren, Judith A. Ouellette et al., "Minority Influence: A Meta-Analytic Review of Social Influence Processes, *Psychological Bulletin* 115, no. 3 (May 1994): 323-345.

"Now I want all you people": Ricky Riccardi, *What a Wonderful World: The Magic of Louis Armstrong's Later Years* (New York: Pantheon, 2011), 281.

9 Body and Soul

"life wasn't worth": Teachout, *Pops*, 356.
"Doc, that's all right": Ibid., 367.
"When I pick up that horn": Ibid., 22.
"First comes my horn": Bergreen, *An Extravagant Life*, 421.
"I never tried to prove nothing": Albin Krebs, "Louis Armstrong, Jazz Trumpeter and Singer, Dies," *New York Times*, July 7, 1971.
"Happiness lies at the intersection": Jen Angel, "10 Things Science Says Will Make You Happy," *Yes!* www.yesmagazine.org/issues/sustainable-happiness/10-things-science-says-will-make-you (accessed August 2011).
"Pops loved to play": Teachout, *Pops*, 348.
"You ever give me a night off": Riccardi, *What a Wonderful World*, 244-245.
Clarinetist Joe Darensbourg: Ibid., 211.

10 What a Wonderful World

Record producer Bob Thiele: Teachout, *Pops*, 351.
The head of the label: Riccardi, *What a Wonderful World*, 260.
"a smile that came from within": "Reliving the Legend of Louis Armstrong," *CNN.com*, http://premium.asia.cnn.com/TRANSCRIPTS/0108/04/smn.16.html (accessed June 2012).
"My whole life": Teachout, *Pops*, 379.
"People love me": Giddins, *Satchmo*, 83.
spending twenty dollars: Dacher Keltner, *Born to Be Good* (W. W. Norton & Company, 2009), 5.
In an experiment: Frans de Waal, "The Evolution of Empathy," *Greater Good*, http://greatergood.berkeley.edu/article/item/the_evolution_of_empathy (accessed June 2012).
They get their soul lifted: Riccardi, *What a Wonderful World*, 306.
George Avakian said: "Reliving the Legend," CNN.
Late in Louis's life: Ward and Burns, *Jazz*, 453.
"I've had a beautiful life": Riccardi, *What a Wonderful World*, 281.
"I'm too busy thinking": Michael Rosenberg, "We All Have a Shot at Happiness," *Detroit Free Press*, http://www.freep.com/article/20120518/COL22/205180431/michael-rosenberg-ford-field-elevator (accessed May 2012).

"What is the use": "Quotes Falsely Attributed," *Winston Churchill Centre and Museum*, http://www.winstonchurchill .org/learn/speeches/quotations/quotes-falsely-attributed (accessed June 2012).

Coda

And all I'm saying: Louis Armstrong, spoken introduction to "What a Wonderful World," *Louis Armstrong and His Friends*, LP 6369401, Phillips, 1970.

Photographs

Frontispiece: Herman Hiller, *New York World-Telegram & Sun*, 1953, public domain.
73: *New York World-Telegram & Sun*, 1953, public domain.
97: Joseph P. Gottlieb, 1946, public domain.
134: Joseph P. Gottlieb, 1947, public domain.
168: Original image by "Hephaestos," *Wikimedia Commons*, http://commons.wikimedia.org/wiki/File: BlueberryiBook.jpeg (accessed July 2012), Creative Commons Attribution-Share Alike 3.0 license.

About the Author

Phil Lynch is author of the motivational blog UpTeach (upteach.blogspot.com), the leading site of encouragement for educators. He holds a degree in psychology from the University of Michigan and a master's degree in history from Fort Hays State University, Kansas. A former United Methodist youth pastor, Phil is a psychology and social studies instructor with over twenty years' experience helping students reach their potential in the Escanaba, Michigan, public schools.

Phil is also a lifelong musician, having received in high school – as a bit of foreshadowing – the Louis Armstrong Jazz Award. In his spare time he's a semi-professional jazz pianist scouring the back-woods of Michigan's Upper Peninsula for gigs with his trio. He resides in Escanaba, on the north shore of Lake Michigan, with his wife and four children.

Made in the USA
Monee, IL
10 January 2022

87654505R00104